YOU DON'T NEED
PERMISSION

YOU DON'T NEED PERMISSION

Finding your path to a purely authentic life

Christina Ellis

gatekeeper press™
Columbus, Ohio

You Don't Need Permission: Finding your path to a purely authentic life
Published by Gatekeeper Press
2167 Stringtown Rd, Suite 109
Columbus, OH 43123-2989
www.GatekeeperPress.com

The editorial work for this book is entirely the product of the author. Gatekeeper Press did not participate in and is not responsible for any aspect of this element.

Library of Congress Control Number: 2020949168
ISBN (hardcover):
ISBN (paperback): 9781662906077
eISBN: 9781662906084

Dedication

This book is dedicated to all the women in my life. I have been lucky enough to be surrounded by strong women who have taught me numerous lessons—sometimes more than I wanted. Generations before me and after me—seemed to converge as wise sages to help me toddle my way through life.

To the women before me who defined what it meant to be tough and independent, who carried the sacred torch, and provided lessons by virtue of their own life. To my dear friends who have held my hand and walked part or all of the path with me. To my mother who was an unexpected guide on the tumultuous road with me. To my daughters who are the love and light of my life.

This book is my gratitude for each and every one of you, for all of the hard-won lessons, and reflections of imperfect love. I am proud to have been raised to not ask for permission.

Contents

Prologue

I want to tell you about my "IT" moment. These days, I truly loathe telling this story. Nonetheless, I would have never written this book if IT hadn't happened to me. And, in order for you to gain trust in me and the things I have to say about taking life by the horns, you have to know where I came from. So here it goes.

It was a day I will never forget; it was a Friday morning. My youngest daughter, Sydney, was still in high school but was home due to a teacher in-service day. I jumped at the chance to get some time with her and bribed her into spending the morning with me by going to our favorite breakfast joint. My spouse (who I had been with for the past four years building an idyllic life together) had just gotten home from traveling for work and happily opted for some time alone.

During breakfast with Syd, I turned off my phone and put it away so as to focus on her. When I turned it back on two hours later, there were numerous missed calls and frantic, choppy text messages. My spouse had been arrested and taken from our home in handcuffs.

My head was spinning. I couldn't think straight to save my life. I drove all over town to each of the city, county, and state jails, asking for any crumbs of information, as if my spouse had checked into a Hilton and I could simply pop in for a visit.

Completely confused and unable to get any useful information, I drove home. When I got there, my house was entirely blocked off with yellow crime scene tape and a dozen detectives were turning my home and my life upside down.

When I pulled up, I was met by three detectives who immediately keyed in on me and presented me with a warrant. They notified me that the love of my life had been arrested and charged with *murder*. My whole entire world began to spin . . . faster and faster. I couldn't breathe. I couldn't think. I couldn't stand.

It was the biggest gut punch I had ever experienced. How could this be? Why didn't I see it? How could someone I loved so deeply be capable of such a thing? And who was I that I picked this person to share my life with? Hours later, as I laid on the kitchen floor in the fetal position crying, I could not imagine how I got there.

The next six months were spent caught up in a legal system that I did not understand, nor had any experience with. I searched for the best representation, hoping there was a mistake or misunderstanding that would be an impetus for an immediate release. Financial and emotional ruin were handed to me swiftly. I tried to protect my daughters, family, and friends but I was a shell of a human and could barely function. I was not able to be the strong one, the person I had always prided myself on being.

After the final guilty verdict came down, I filed for divorce, sold our home, and went on a soul-searching journey for the next four years. I didn't understand this "thing" that had come into my life, turned it inside out, and left it ravaged. I did not understand any of it, but I desperately needed to find my way back.

I questioned life. I cried. I yelled. I was pissed. I was beyond hurt. I was nursing an open wound. I cried some more, for a long time . . . four years to be exact. I began to relish in the fact that I had been so damaged and was still standing. It became a big part of who I was. And then I realized that it actually wasn't about me or at least it did not have to be going forward. Nor did I want it to be. It is not how I wanted to define myself.

That said, the pity, the condolences, the hugs from others, became my lifeline. In some ways, they comforted me to the extent that I found I needed it and craved it. I had fallen into the sad reality of willingly giving up control of my life and destiny for the crumbs of others' compassion.

My confidence had left me and I relied entirely upon others to make me feel better. All they saw was that I was still standing—as if standing was the goal. They had no idea how broken I was yet, nonetheless, their words and condolences comforted me.

The problem with that is I couldn't count on what, when, or how much of their attention I would receive. I couldn't give myself what I needed and relied on "them" to give that to me. It was a self-perpetuating downward spiral, with no end in sight. It is from the bottom of that spiral that the inspiration for this book came about.

When I was mired in it, however, it was my comfort zone. Yes, I said it. My victimhood became my comfort (there's a whole chapter on that later in this book). It was a great method for getting that attention from others. A great reason not to function. A great reason, some mornings, not to get out of bed at all. A great reason for me to fail. I often describe this period of my life as the time that "it" happened to me. It was my story. It was my downfall. It was my excuse. It was, at the time, my reason for being.

Throughout the rest of this book, to the extent I reference this story at all, I'm going to refer to it simply as "my IT moment." I won't go there very often—but when I do, you'll know what I'm talking about.

A couple more words about this book before you dig in. When it comes to my communication style, I'm a very "what you see is what you get" kind of person. I won't mince words. I will swear sometimes. I will talk to you like I talk to my best friend. After all, something prompted you to pick up a book titled *You Don't Need Permission*.

The pull of that phrase is something that you and I share on an intimate level. I'm fortunate enough to be at that point in life where I absolutely live the principles of this book every day. But it was a long, hard battle getting to this point. My sincere hope is that in sharing my experiences and lessons with you, you can get to your happy place much more quickly and efficiently than I did.

Before we dive too deep, however, I guess I should tell you a few more things about me. After all, why should you read a whole book written by some woman whose only credential is having lived through a tragedy? If that were the only experience needed to dispense the type of wisdom I'm about to throw at you, at least 75% of the women you know would be moments away from giving their own TED talk (actually, I wish all of them *would* do that). But I digress . . .

In addition to going through some stuff (believe me, you'll get plenty of other, smaller "it" moments as we go through this book together), I've also had the great fortune of helping other people live their best lives for over 25 years. Early on, I started a successful career in business development, marketing, and sales. My secret to success was that I was constantly working on making *myself* a better person—rather than being a corporate brown-noser or doing the same, tired things everyone else in my field did. As a result, people began asking me about my "secret sauce"—and I began to share it with them. Hence, for the past decade-plus, I have worked as a business coach who doesn't give a rat's ass about my client's businesses (ok, that might be an overstatement meant to get your attention). Instead, I focus on the individuals behind the dollar signs and am proud to say that methodology has led my clients to some phenomenal results—both personally and professionally.

Through the years, many of my clients have asked me to write this book. Because I tend to keep my business and private life separate, those folks have no idea what they're in for. For this book to be authentic, however, it really had to be an intentional blending of my *whole* life. And it is. Ultimately, I believe that if I was able to make this life work as beautifully as it has—on all levels—you can too. So, let's stop talking about me and start in on *your* life's journey.

Take a deep breath.

Exhale.

Good. Let's get started.

"The question isn't who is going to let me; it's who is going to stop me."

~Ayn Rand

One

Living with Intention

When I decided to write this book, that quote echoed in my brain. Over the course of the last decade, my life has changed dramatically. No longer do I live a life charted by the expectations of others. The reason for this is simple—I made a conscious decision to live with intention.

It may surprise you to hear that nothing *external* to my life has changed. I still have kids, a new relationship, a job, bills to pay, friendships to nurture, and organizations I support. People still ask me to do things for them and with them. The difference comes in how I approach these things. Today, when I decide to spend my time doing something . . . anything . . . my decision is deliberate. And my life has never been better.

The unique expectations on women

Let me be clear from the outset. This book is largely written for women. It's not that I don't think the central premise of the book—*you don't need permission*—isn't helpful to men. It undoubtedly is. The truth, however, is that men and women grow up very differently in our society. Like it or not (and despite all our attempts at modernity), women are expected to sacrifice more of their time in service to others. Those expectations are piled on from a very young age.

A friend of mine recently told me an illustrative story about how female-specific expectations invaded her life early on. She grew up in one of those middle-class, suburban American families where holidays were a time for the whole family to get together. All the grandparents, aunts, uncles, cousins, second-cousins, in-laws, and unrelated stragglers would gather at one house for Thanksgiving, Christmas, and other sacrosanct holidays like the Super Bowl.

My friend came out of the womb a die-hard tomboy. From the time she had a say in what she wanted to do, she played baseball, rode bikes, shunned dresses, and (her words, not mine) destroyed all Barbie-related paraphernalia people were stupid enough to give her. She hung out with boys at school, detested all things pink, and generally misunderstood girls.

Despite her more masculine-leaning interests, my friend got an early lesson in gender expectations during one of those family get togethers. As she tells it, the realization hit on Thanksgiving when she was six or seven years old.

Her family arrived at Grandma's house in the morning. As usual, her mom and sister, armed with bags of groceries, headed straight for the kitchen. My friend followed her dad and brothers into the living room where they would all take a spot near Grandpa's recliner to watch football.

"Jenny," her mom screeched, "where do you think you're going? Get back in this kitchen and help us peel potatoes!"

"But Mom," she whined, "I wanna watch football with Grandpa."

"Young lady, you get in here right now and get to work!"

The dialogue continued with my friend questioning why neither of her brothers had to take up residence in the kitchen. "Because" was the best reasoning her mom would provide. As the day progressed and more relatives arrived, Jenny noticed that all females went straight to the kitchen while all men drank beer and watched football in the comfort of the living room.

The lesson was clear: girls/women simply have different expectations when it comes to the use of their time. Buy the groceries, cook the meals, clean the dishes, do the laundry, change the diapers, drive the kids to practice, nurture your sick husband, make cookies for the bake sale, volunteer at the hospital, buy school clothes, tuck the kids in at night. Oh, and in today's society, you ladies should also hold down a full-time job because we all need that second income.

The long and short of it is that if there's a task to be undertaken that involves caretaking, women are expected to handle it 90% of the time. I'm not saying that this is right or wrong. What I am saying is that this state of affairs leads women to live without intention more often than not. Over time, in fact, we learn to subsume our own thoughts and desires to such an extent that we wake up one morning and find ourselves crushed by the weight of expectation. It happened to me in a way I never expected.

The first time life taught me to live with intention

In life, I have learned there are many moments when—if we are paying attention—lessons are waiting for us. Life is not meant to be made of days running through daisy fields with unicorns and birds singing above our heads. It is the gritty, nasty crap of life that holds the gifts for our learning pleasure. I am sure your life is made up of many such opportunities for advancement. My "IT moment," as described in the Prologue, was undoubtedly important for this book to come to fruition. Yet, it was a different run-in with reality that *first* allowed me to realize how incredibly important living with intention is. In fact, I would be disingenuous if I didn't credit this earlier experience for prompting my near-obssession with time and intention. Here's what happened:

The news of my abnormal mammogram results didn't faze me at all. I had dense, lumpy breasts. So what? We already knew this. More than anything, I was annoyed that my doctor was forcing me to come back for an ultrasound so quickly. It had taken them two months to schedule my mammogram in the first place. I figured we could wait another two or three months for the follow-up test.

"No, Christina. The doctor insists you come back immediately." The nurse sounded so serious. Despite my irritation, my field of vision suddenly constricted into a narrow tunnel. What was the rush? As my vision returned to normal, I relented, scheduled an ultrasound for a couple days later, and went back to feeling more annoyed than worried. I didn't tell anyone that I needed a follow-up test.

On the day of the ultrasound, I was in a good mood. I was going to prove them wrong. This wasn't how I was going to go out. I had lumpy breasts, for shit's sake. I reminded the ultrasound tech of this as she started the procedure. To cut the deafening silence in the room, I started making jokes. This was no big deal. Why was she acting like it was? She didn't even crack a smile . . . and trust me, my jokes are good!

Finally, I asked her. "What do you see in there?"

"I'm not supposed to say anything to you," she replied, stoically.

"Well, that's a dead giveaway," I replied, as my nerves started to reveal themselves.

She wasn't having it. "The doctor will be contacting you."

No problem. I was sure my doctor would be thrilled to give me the good news when she finally got around to calling me in a week or two. The call came just a few hours later.

"Christina, we need to get you in now for a biopsy."

That was the moment. That was the singular moment in my life that led me to start thinking about things like time and intentionality in a whole new way. I didn't even realize it then. In that moment, all I could think about was the fact that I had decisions to make. What was going to happen to my two girls, then aged 3 and 7? How would my family survive this? Did I need to start making plans? What was happening to me? I didn't break down, cry, or even bother anyone else with the news. I just started thinking about what needed to be done.

On the day of the biopsy, the doctor was adamant that they remove the entire tumor during that procedure. This was suddenly getting very real. Nevertheless, all I could think about as the tumor was extracted was my youngest daughter's bedroom.

I am an artist, so when my kids were old enough, I let them pick out a theme for their rooms and then I painted their entire room to match their chosen theme. My older daughter, Taylor, wanted to live underwater. For her, I created an ocean scene filled with fish, seaweed, and shells. My three-year-old, Sydney, had only recently been able to articulate her choice: bugs. She loved bugs. So, naturally, I started painting her room with flowers holding every kind of bug you can imagine. But her room was only halfway done on the day of the biopsy. And suddenly, my singular focus was the fact that I had to finish that room.

I held it together until the biopsy was finished. Afterwards, I drove home, walked into my house, and completely lost it. I let myself cry for a short while and then I became a woman possessed. I had to paint. I had to get all of my painting supplies out and I had to finish Syd's room now. I painted furiously. What mattered in that moment more than anything else was . . . bugs. Hours later, my husband came home and found me crying and painting bugs.

Without waiting for his inquisition, I simply looked up at him and said, "I'm gonna die and I need to finish this room." I had put off painting Syd's bugs so I could cook and clean and run errands and keep our household in order—all the things that were expected of me. On that day, I threw all of those expectations out the window. Without realizing it, being faced with death had forced me into an intentional life.

I was one of the lucky ones. The biopsy results were negative, and I got to resume normalcy. Well, normal except for the fact that I was never again going to let other people's expectations stop me from doing things like painting bugs or living life on my own terms.

Easing into an intentional life by being intentional about time

I wish I could tell you that immediately after my breast cancer scare, I began living a purely intentional life. That wouldn't be the truth. I did finish painting Syd's room. After that, however, I went right back to cooking and cleaning and meeting everyone else's expectations but my own. Fortunately, that experience planted a seed in my soul that would germinate, bud, and blossom over the course of a decade. Let's hope we can speed up that process for you.

It all starts with being intentional about time.

Now, correct me if I'm wrong, but you only have 24 hours in a day, right? You don't get more than me and I don't get more than you. In fact, in a recent documentary called *Inside Bill's Brain: Decoding Bill Gates*, one of the Microsoft billionaire's longtime colleagues noted that despite all his money and fame, he still only gets the same 1,440 minutes a day that the rest of us get. The difference between Bill Gates and most other people, however, is that he is incredibly intentional about time.

For one of the world's richest men, time intentionality manifests in things like never being late to meetings, reading multiple books during flights and on vacation, and taking advantage of small breaks between other scheduled tasks to be productive (for example, answering emails in the five minutes between meetings rather than scrolling through Facebook). For you, time intentionality might actually *include* scrolling through Facebook during small breaks because you realize you need to turn off your brain from time to time in order to remain sharp.

That's fine. Time intentionality is not a judgment about *how* you use your time. Rather, it is about being *thoughtful* about how you use your time.

Once you make that decision to be intentional, you can start to get rid of the things that overwhelm your life. I understand that you've been groomed to be a hero—the kind of person who has time for everyone and everything. You probably feel guilty telling other people "no." Or perhaps you still believe in the concept of "multitasking." That's not realistic. Consider multitasking as something that went away with neon, Ferris Bueller, and cassette tapes.

When it comes to that precious resource—your limited time—you absolutely cannot be all things to all people. Nor should you want to be. In order to get over your hero complex, you're going to have to shift your mindset. This isn't a minor adjustment. In order to switch from being overwhelmed to being in control, you have to stop letting other people fill your time and start taking responsibility for it. This is a difficult process because life has conditioned you to stay busy. Let me explain.

Do you remember those math worksheets they used to give you in grade school? Most of the time, you'd get three or four sheets to complete during math time. Being the genius that you are, you would finish 15 to 20 minutes early. You would excitedly raise your hand, expecting the teacher to heap praise on you for your stunning brilliance. But instead of getting praise, what did you get? If your teacher was anything like mine, you'd get a couple more worksheets and a warning for you to remain silent until the period was over.

BAM! You just got hit with a life lesson! In that moment, you learned that your value came from completing busy work rather than performing higher-level, creative thinking. Sadly, it's not just other people who are teaching our kids this lesson. We do it as parents every day. For example, rather than being allowed to play after school, many kids today are schlepped from one activity to another. Gymnastics, dance, soccer, baseball, music lessons, debate team. Then, when they get home, they have to practice all of those things so they can be the best at them. If they're not, they can be ostracized or bullied. By perpetuating this paradigm, we're feeding into the message that personal value comes not from happiness, but from being busy to appease others.

As adults, this translates into a life where we still only feel valuable if we keep busy all day long. In fact, the more stressed out we are, the better. That's the measure of success, right? Ultimately, this conditioning has transformed us into a bunch of adults who can't walk down the street without also staring at our phones for fear that someone will think we're not busy. Oh, the shame!

As moms, we tell ourselves that we're not good at mothering unless we're filling every moment in service to our children. We wake them up, we get them dressed, and we make their food for the day. Then we drive them from home to school to practice to social events and then back home again. Once we're home, we make sure they're doing their homework, brushing their teeth, and not being corrupted by television and social media. We make costumes for the school play and, in our spare time, volunteer to chaperone their field trips. And if we don't do every single one of these things, we're not keeping busy which means we're not doing a good job, which means we're feeling shame again. It's exhausting just thinking about it.

Of course, some mothers can't do that. Some have to work two or three jobs just to put food on the table. Despite how busy they are, they still get shamed for not doing enough. For not volunteering enough. For not baking enough cookies for the stupid bake sale. This shame and blame mentality has to stop.

So, how do we accomplish that? Intentionality is the key. Now that you can see that the "busy conditioning" was placed in your mind by someone else, you can take steps to remove it and replace it with healthier ways of relating to time and organization. There was probably a time in your life when you could sit and play (the work of a child) all day. You may have been consumed by one task, living in a world of your own creation. Your focus and creativity are not gone, they have just been covered up by other people's expectations, false rules, and misguided shame.

I'm not advocating that you stop doing things for others so you can simply play all day. Instead, realize that it is your job as an adult to be aware of how often you are guided by others' priorities. Now that you have the knowledge, you have to take responsibility. Stop making excuses, stop giving all of your power and time to others, stop putting yourself second, third, fourth, or worse. Stop saying that you "have" to do something. All decisions are your own. From this day forward, you get to say that you "choose" to do things. How you spend your time is an intentional decision that you will make from here on out. You are being handed the keys to the kingdom. Use them wisely for your benefit and gain.

One way to begin this process of reclaiming your time is to understand the difference between caring and caretaking. As women, we're taught that we're supposed to care about others. In fact, for most of us, caring comes very naturally (especially if you have children). The problem comes in when we subconsciously switch from caring to care-taking. Let me explain the difference.

When we're caring for others, we are simply expressing our love and support for them. Care can be expressed in a variety of ways, including doing things for the people we love. So, what is the difference? It comes down to one word . . . responsibility. Who has it and what is going to come of it? When we care about someone, we want to support them, teach them, guide them, and be there for them through the challenges.

When we are caretaking, on the other hand, we are taking on someone else's responsibility, and removing the discomfort of the learning curve for them. We carry the responsibility of achieving the end result. Essentially, we have taken away the gift of learning from them as a way to ease their pain of not knowing. In truth, we have robbed them of the gift of growth, however ugly that growth path may be. Let me give you an example.

Most of us start to teach our kids to tie their own shoes at around age four or five. They stumble and bumble and generally take longer than you ever imagined just to accomplish this simple task (hence the popularity of Velcro shoes for children).

Imagine a busy mom. She's got 20,000 things to get done in her day and she needs to get her three-year-old dressed so she can put him in the car and get to the grocery store. "Johnny," she says, "please tie your shoes so we can go." Twenty minutes later, there's Johnny, on the floor, still fumbling with his laces. What does she do? She ties his shoes for him. Over the course of the next incredibly busy month, she does the same thing at least 50 times. She always seems to be rushing and so she just takes care of the problem for him. She is literally care-taking.

The byproduct of this, of course, is that she has taken away Johnny's responsibility for learning to tie his own shoes. As the months go by, she continues to take up her time doing this menial task that Johnny needs to learn to do for himself. You want to be tying Johnny's shoes as he heads off to prom? No? I didn't think so. Put the responsibility back on Johnny, and his girlfriend will thank you for it.

Of course, women do some version of this every single day. We do the family's laundry rather than teaching the kids (and spouse) to do it for themselves. We cook the meals rather than showing the people we care about how to prepare nutritious food. In fact, we get so caught up in caretaking, that we forget to take responsibility for our own time.

What I'm really advocating here is that you start asking yourself, as you perform services for those around you, whether you are caring or caretaking. If the answer is the latter, it is time to start being intentional about *your* time.

You know what will happen when you stop spending all of your time purely in service of others? Those people will start giving you a level of respect you never imagined. They may have to do some things for themselves, but they'll be better for it. Meanwhile, you will begin to lose the crushing weight of their expectations. You can, in fact, choose to spend some of your time on you.

I can almost hear the chorus of excuses rushing my way.

"But I have a three-year-old! How's she supposed to get to preschool if I don't take her?"

"But my husband doesn't know how to cook!"

"But my partner makes so much more money than me. Shouldn't I take care of all the household tasks?"

Whoa, Martha Stewart! If you're asking those questions, go back and read the chapter again. There is no good or bad way to spend your time. I'm only advocating that you're intentional about your use of time. So, if you want to drive your three-year-old to preschool, cook dinner for your husband, or perform extra household tasks, go for it! Just be sure that you are doing so intentionally.

What may happen when you decide to use your time intentionally is that other solutions come to you. Perhaps you can join a carpool to get the kids around. Maybe your husband will learn to cook a few of his favorite meals on his own. Maybe the laundry will only get done on the weekends.

But you know what else may happen? You may have time to bring creativity back into your life. You may carve out a few hours a week to spend time by yourself . . . taking a bath, reading a magazine, or otherwise recharging your batteries. You may have a meal cooked for you. You won't know until you make the decision to be intentional.

Many of you are probably looking for time management tips here. I could give you those, but that would happen in an entirely different book. Instead, I'm going to give you examples of how being intentional with your time can change your life entirely.

In my coaching business, I have a client who runs a fairly successful garment manufacturing business. During one of our weekly calls, she sounded exasperated. Naturally, I asked what was wrong.

"Ugh," she replied. "I have this employee who is a really nice guy, but he is just so *needy*. I like him, but he is constantly asking for advances on payroll. Then, after I give him an advance, he calls in sick and I have to find a replacement each time. When he does come to work, he wants to talk my ear off about his personal problems. He just has me feeling completely exhausted."

I think she was surprised by my reply: "You do realize, don't you, that this is all your fault?"

After a brief gasp and an almost-uncomfortable pause, she came back with, "I guess you're right. I guess I'm enabling him."

"Guess again," I said. "This isn't about him. It's about YOU. You are choosing to spend your time dealing with his problems and the fallout that they create. If you were being intentional about your time, you'd fire him. That would free up all the time you're wasting on him so you could spend it on your business." She reluctantly agreed and we went on to discuss other aspects of her company.

The following week, she sounded much more upbeat. "You were right!" she exclaimed. I wasn't surprised. It turns out that even though she "felt bad" about firing him, the mere fact of prioritizing her own time over his problems was a godsend. She had quickly replaced the guy with one of the temps she always called when he didn't come to work. That person showed up, did the work assigned to her, and went home. Meanwhile, my client had time to solve some accounting problems, make branding decisions, and generally move her business forward. All of that came from simply choosing to be intentional about her time.

Another client is a popular massage therapist who also happens to be a yoga instructor. We had discussed the topic of the intentionality of time generally, but never in the context of her business. One day she called me well ahead of her next scheduled coaching session. Haha, nope, I would not let that happen! That would be caretaking by allowing a client to step on my time. See how I snuck that in there? Actually, she called me on her next regularly-scheduled appointment time with wonderful news.

"I just wanted to share with you how I took that whole time-intentionality thing to heart," she said. It turns out that she had several massage clients who had significant muscular ailments but would complain that they couldn't afford to have more than one massage per month at her normal rate of $125 per hour. "I wanted to help them more," she explained, "but I can't lower my rate every time someone wants more frequent massages. If I did, I'd quickly go out of business."

She decided (quite on her own, I might add) to apply time-intentionality to the problem. She realized that she hadn't done much with the yin yoga teaching certification that she had obtained a year prior. (For those of you who aren't familiar with the practice, yin yoga is a slow-paced style of yoga where participants hold various stretches for one to five minutes—great for stretching out sore muscles). She also realized that she had enough space in her office to teach up to 10 yoga students at a time. That's when the idea hit her.

"I realized that if I held yin yoga classes a couple times a week, my clients could maintain the muscular benefit they gained from my massages between their regular appointments. The price of the class is just $35 per hour. That means that as often as they want, they can help themselves maintain health for $90 less than it would cost to get a massage. Meanwhile, every time I hold a class for 10 students, I earn $350 in that hour as opposed to the $125 I would earn by giving a massage."

From a math perspective, she bought herself almost two hours of free time every time she held a yin yoga class. Her clients felt like they were getting a deal and she freed up extra time to work on her business. Intentionality of time is a powerful thing.

I see this all the time in my work as a business coach. What I suggest to my clients, and what I'm suggesting to you now, is to go back in time to your third-grade math class. Imagine the different lessons you would have learned about time if your teacher, instead of handing you more worksheets when you finished the first batch, asked you to go outside, think quietly about what you wanted your life to look like, and then asked you to write a short paragraph about your dreams.

What you may have learned in that moment is how to live with intention—how to live a life based on the time you took to dream about ideals. And you would have a written vision, albeit crude but nevertheless valuable, of how you wanted your life to look. A roadmap or blueprint for you to follow rather than willy-nilly fulfilling others' expectations of you.

When I ask my coaching clients to take time each day to dream about what their perfect life would look like, their lives (business and personal) tend to change dramatically. In order to live with intentionality surrounding time, we have to give ourselves this critical quiet time to dream.

Without it, we can get so caught up in caretaking for others that we fail to take care of ourselves. I'd like you to put the book down for a moment and really think about this. Carve out a time in your day when you can spend 10 minutes dreaming. Then do it for a week and see what happens.

Living an intentional life

Once you begin being intentional about your time, intentionality starts to become addictive. You'll find yourself wanting more and, most importantly, you'll find yourself *getting* more. And, because intentionality of time often involves prioritizing your*self*, you'll start to see that intentionality bleeds into everything you do.

As I began drafting notes for this book, I started talking about the concept of intentionality with several of the people close to me. I found these conversations to be incredibly useful as an author, but never really considered that my friends and loved ones would benefit from them. And then I got a call from my friend Sarah.

Sarah is in her late forties and, by all accounts, is living a rather intentional life. She gave up a lucrative legal career to pursue art full time. She abandoned the societal pressure to have big cars, big houses, and big debt for a simple life filled with simple pleasures and the pursuit of creativity. The model of intention, right?

Almost. While Sarah was leading an intentional life career-wise, she was doing the exact opposite in her relationships. Her 13-year marriage had ended in her late thirties and, after that, she never quite found "the one." What she did do is become a chameleon. Every time she started a new relationship, she became a version of herself that reflected the person she was dating. If they liked baseball, she liked baseball. If they liked to go out dancing, she would swallow her inner introvert and head out to a dance club. She often found herself feeling anxious, insecure, and unfulfilled. Yet she kept trying.

The pinnacle of this unhealthy relationship pattern happened when Sarah met someone, fell in love, and six months later, moved halfway across the country to be with that person. Shortly after she arrived, and anxious to start a "great" relationship, her partner revealed a startling truth:

"I love you but I would like to be ethically non-monogamous."

The truth that Sarah revealed to no one was that that statement was horrifying to her. She loved this person . . . how could they want to be with other people? Rather than expressing her horror, however, Sarah sucked it up. She said she'd try it out. And, like a good non-monogamous girlfriend, she signed up for dating apps in her new city and tried to make a go of it. Meanwhile, she listened to all sorts of stories about the fun her partner was having with other people. It crushed her spirit.

For weeks, Sarah never let on how miserable she was. She was a modern woman. This had to work. If she just tried hard enough, she could accept it, right? Eventually, she'd start having fun in this lifestyle, right? While all her friends told her to run for the hills, Sarah stuck it out.

Then her partner left town for three weeks on a business trip. The time and distance allowed her to do some deep thinking. Fortunately, she remembered our talks about intentionality. What she realized was that while being non-monogamous (ethically or not) might work for some people, it did not work for her. She also realized that this wasn't a situation that called for anger or judgment. After all, her partner had been truthful and upfront about the whole situation. There was no deception. This just wasn't a life Sarah would ever *intentionally* choose to lead. And that, she decided, was ok.

Of course, when her partner returned from the business trip, he was unusually attentive. He had missed her and realized while away just how much he loved her. Sarah was quickly pulled back in. That is, she was pulled back in until three days later when he took off to spend time with another of his paramours.

Much to her surprise, Sarah didn't feel hurt. She simply felt intentional. She sent a text that said, "Hey, I meant to talk to you about this when you returned but we haven't had time yet. I decided while you were gone that this isn't a life I want to lead. I know you're not doing anything wrong and I'm not judging you but I'm also not willing to do this anymore. I love you and wish you the best, but this is where it ends for me."

As she hit "Send," Sarah didn't expect to hear from him again. And she was actually ok with that. She was going to hold out for a life that was intentionally awesome.

What happened next, however, did surprise her. Instead of carelessly continuing things with the other woman, he instantly drove back to Sarah's door. The two of them talked, she held her boundaries, and he committed to a monogamous relationship. In fact, he said he actually respected Sarah more than ever for holding her line.

By the time Sarah and I talked, several weeks had passed since this exchange. Not surprisingly, everything in her world was different. Her relationship was the one she had always wanted. She respected herself and was getting respect in return.

Meanwhile, this whole notion of living with intention had infected her life. Suddenly, for example, she was no longer offering "deals" to new clients. She simply stated what she was worth, asked for the retainer agreement, and was getting it! Her deliberate intention to value herself had allowed others to value her for what she was worth. The change was immediate and startling.

For you, living an intentional life may look completely different. Maybe you stop accepting negative treatment from a co-worker. Maybe you talk to your partner about taking more camping trips. Whatever your intention looks like, isn't now the time?

Can I promise that every decision to live an intentional life will be as successful as Sarah's? Of course not. For you, the changes may come in small increments, but they will come . . . and the rest of your life will be better for it.

You don't know how much time you have

I want to close this chapter with a simple truth. None of us knows how many more minutes we have to live on this planet. You could be hit by a bus tomorrow—or you could live to be 113. The point is, none of us knows how much time we actually have.

"Memento Mori" is from the stoic philosophy of life. Translated to English, it means "remember, you must die." To many people it is a sad thought . . . unnerving . . . maybe even terrifying! But I am suggesting you use it to inspire yourself to be intentional about your life. To squeeze the most out of your 1,440 minutes.

Every.

Single.

Day.

So, let's engage in one more exercise. Imagine that you did know the exact moment that you were going to die. Now imagine that that moment is exactly one week from today. You would probably live the next week very differently than you would if you still had the chance to live to 113.

For starters, you would probably become dramatically intentional about who you chose to spend your time with. Think about that for a minute. Who would you make sure you talked to? What would you say to them? Would you want them to know the extent of your love? Would you thank them for being a part of your life?

Next, think about what you would do with those people. Would you hug them? Take a trip with them? Have a large gathering they could all attend at once? Would you have that second glass of wine? Would you go to the beach? Picture that last week as having no limits. You can go anywhere, see anyone, and do anything. What would you do?

It's time to put the book down again and really think about how you would spend your last week on Earth.

. . .

Ok, you're back! Good! I have a question for you. When you imagined your last week, did it look very different from the way you're going to spend the next seven days? If so, why? You may not be able to immediately take that trip to Italy that you dreamt about for your last week but certainly you can hug your best friend? Surely you could organize a gathering with all your favorite people? I'm guessing you have time to tell the people you care about that you love them.

I'm not saying that real life should not and will not "get in the way."

We all have jobs to do, bills to pay, and responsibilities to take care of. But again, there are no guarantees about the time we have left here. Once you begin to live an intentional life, every week can look a little more like the last week that you just envisioned. Isn't that a beautiful thought?

"Quote . . ."

Two

Expectations

When I set out to write this book, there was no planned chapter on "Expectations." Nonetheless, as my work on the remainder of the book progressed, I realized that every chapter, in one form or another, had to do with expectations.

It's funny too because, in society, we don't talk about expectations that much. Sure, you might expect your kids to do their homework. Your spouse may expect you to take the garbage out. But those things are automatic. What I found as I worked through the concepts in this book is that expectations—big and small—infiltrate every single aspect of our lives.

It's easy to say that the answer to all of this is to simply "manage your expectations." We've all heard that one, right? And, sure . . . that's a good tactic that we'll talk about. But first, why don't we take a look at what expectations are, where they come from, and how they impact our interactions with others. First, however, I want to share some thoughts on the very concept of expectations.

As you read through the chapters of this book, you'll find that each chapter begins with a quote. Sometimes, they're inspirational. Other times, they're thought-provoking. Some, I had planned well before I started the book. Many were researched as the content developed. This chapter, being a "surprise" chapter that I decided to include toward the end of the writing project, didn't have a pre-planned quote.

Consequently, I set out to find one. And oh, what a letdown that process was! Here's the gist of what I found:

"If you expect nothing from anybody, you're never disappointed." – Sylvia Plath

"Blessed is he who expects nothing, for he shall never be disappointed." – Alexander Pope

"I find my life is a lot easier the lower I keep my expectations." – Bill Watterson

"There were two ways to be happy: improve your reality or lower your expectations." – Jodi Picoult

What fatalistic thinking! While each of these quotes may be grounded in some form of truth, they really miss a lot of the analysis that we need to be doing about expectations. Let me explain.

When do we have expectations?

The answer to this question is: "Literally, every second of every day." Think about it.

When you walk into the grocery store, you expect that the items you intend to purchase will be on the shelves. You expect the floors to be clean and the produce to be fresh. You expect that the prices will be consistent with other stores in the region. And you expect to find plastic produce bags on the roll. Dammit! Why can't they keep those plastic bags on the roll?

When you drive down the highway, you expect that other drivers will respect the rules of the road. You expect that no one will put your life in danger. You expect that they will be sober enough to function. While those things may not always happen, it's safe to say that we, as a society, expect them.

When you pay a professional service provider to assist you (let's say a therapist), you expect that that person will have sufficient training and experience to help you with your problem. You expect that they'll charge a reasonable rate for your particular city and that they'll be committed to doing the job you hired them for.

Those are all reasonable expectations, right? And there are a billion other reasonable expectations that fit right alongside those. So, if we adopt the fatalistic reasoning of the above quotes, our entire world falls apart.

If we "expect nothing" from our grocery store, fellow drivers, and paid professionals, what kind of society do we live in? We might as well forgo things like health department inspections, highway patrol officers, and professional licensure standards. After all, if we "expect nothing," why waste our time and tax dollars with enforcement measures?

The truth is, we all have a set of *reasonable* expectations in life. That's the key word, isn't it—"reasonable"? Even within our everyday examples set forth above, a person could quickly become "unreasonable." For example: (1) someone might expect that their grocery store carry all-organic products AND offer prices 75% lower than any other store in the neighborhood; (2) a driver might expect that all local drivers pass a stunt-driving course before they can legally enter the public roadways; or (3) a patient might expect that a therapist move into their home and take care of every emotional twist as it arises. All of those expectations are objectively unreasonable.

They're also easy to spot when we're talking about "everyday" expectations. It gets tougher when we delve into personal expectations. Before we explore that, however, let's take a look at expectations vis-a-vis their close (but very different) relatives—judgements.

Expectations vs. Judgements

It should be pretty clear by now that we all have a set of expectations in life. That, in and of itself, is perfectly normal. Nonetheless, I think we need to take a moment to distinguish between the expectations you have of other people as opposed to the judgements you might make about them.

As usual, we'll do this using an example. Let's begin with Mary, a 42-year-old woman who was divorced from her husband Jason three years ago. Mary and Jason had a pretty decent marriage until Jason decided that he didn't want to spend the rest of his life chasing "the grind." By that point, he had worked 10 years as an electrical engineer with a large firm, had put in a ton of hours, and had amassed quite a bit of money. By age 40, he wanted to leave the firm, start his own sole proprietorship, and cut his work hours by about 60%. In his newfound free time, he wanted to travel the country in an RV, working remotely any time he found a spot with WiFi.

Jason expected that Mary would join him in this dream. Mary, on the other hand, expected that she and Jason would work as hard as they could for as long as they could at the highest-paying jobs they could get. Her expectation was that they would build a large nest egg and travel when they retired at age 65.

Interestingly, while the couple had often discussed their mutual desire to travel the country in an RV, they had never discussed their relative expectations regarding *when* the adventure would begin.

When Jason quit his job, bought an RV, and brought it home to surprise Mary for her 38th birthday, she did not react with joy, as he expected. Rather, she had a complete meltdown about the financial jeopardy she felt Jason was putting them in. It was a fight of such grand proportions that the two never recovered. They divorced a year later.

After the divorce was final, Mary would often tell her friends that she left Jason because he was a "lazy bum." She described him as "lacking motivation" and accused him of being a "drifter." For his part, Jason described Mary as a "tightwad and a gold-digger" who "could never let loose and just have fun."

Do you see what just happened there? Before their big blowout, Mary and Jason each had uncommunicated expectations from the other. After the blowout and the divorce, the pair turned those unmet expectations into nasty judgements about the other.

Now, there's nothing inherently wrong with either Mary's or Jason's expectations (except, perhaps, that they were never communicated fully). Each person was entitled to take ownership of their respective expectations, to prioritize those expectations in their lives, and live life in a way that aligned with those expectations.

Where the two ran into trouble was when they turned their *unmet* expectations into judgement of the other person. Terms like "lazy" or "tightwad" weren't actually fair to either of them. Jason wasn't inherently lazy and Mary wasn't inherently uptight. What they both were, however, was terribly bad at communicating their authentic expectations. And, when they both found those expectations unmet, they turned into judge, jury, and executioner.

My point is this: it's not fair of you to have expectations of someone else that you fail to communicate. And, if you do miss that critical step, it is certainly not fair of you to turn the failed expectations *that belong to you (and only you)*, into criticism of someone else. Your job is to own your expectations and to communicate them. It is not your job to put those expectations onto somebody's else's shoulders.

Please keep this distinction in mind as we begin to explore how our expectations impact our personal relationships. Also, I want you to start thinking about expectations and judgements that you've made in your own life. In particular, if you've had a relationship that failed (again . . . any kind of personal relationship), ask yourself whether you let your uncommunicated expectations turn into unfair judgement. If so, well, there's probably nothing we can do about that now.

The good news, however, is that we can talk about how you might communicate in the future in a way that fosters—rather than destroys—your relationships.

How we form expectations with those closest to us

When we begin to explore the expectations we carry with respect to the people in our lives who are closest to us, the waters get a little bit murkier and the expectations get a little more complex. Let's set up another three examples and then we'll explore a series of questions about each:

1. Megan and Jenny are 21-year-old college students who are best friends and roommates;

2. Tom and Brenda have been married for 10 years;

3. Sonya and Mark have worked closely together in a law office for four years.

Let's take these in order, starting with Megan and Jenny. Megan was raised in a small town with six sisters. She feels very strong ties to God and family and has hopes of meeting her eventual husband at college. Jenny, on the other hand, is an only child from Philadelphia. Her parents were both political activists and she was raised to always speak her mind, regardless of the outcome. Despite their differences, Megan and Jenny have a strong bond and hope to build a lifetime of friendship. Nonetheless, they each had some expectations coming into their situation, none of which were communicated before problems arose.

Jenny, never having had a sister, expected her best friend to be on call for her every need. Meanwhile, Megan, having six sisters, believed that young women can be overly emotional, should rely solely on their family for emotional support, and found Jenny's neediness to be excessive.

Jenny expected her best friend to spend every weekend night with her, while Megan expected that weekends were reserved for dates with potential husbands.

Megan expected Jenny to keep the same level of cleanliness in the girls' apartment that she had to maintain in her childhood home. Jenny, on the other hand, viewed college as a time to "let loose" and didn't much worry about the trappings of domesticity.

As the relationship began to break down, Megan started referring to Jenny as co-dependent, needy, and sloppy. Jenny, meanwhile, called Megan uncaring, slutty, and uptight. Megan's and Jenny's respective expectations certainly shaped the outcome of the friendship. But let's ask a few questions about the situation:

While each woman's expectations were undoubtedly unmet, were they *unreasonable*?

If the expectation was not unreasonable, could the outcome have been changed if the expectation was communicated before a problem arose?

When was the appropriate time to communicate about expectations?

How would communicating the expectation have impacted the overall friendship?

At what point did expectations turn into judgement? Was the transition fair?

* * *

As for Tom and Brenda, well, they met in college and they immediately hit it off. Tom was in a band but was studying to become an engineer. Brenda was a sociology major who planned to become a counselor. The two married shortly after graduation, with grand plans of traveling the world and reaching great success in their respective professions. Ten years into marriage, some problems arose that stemmed from uncommunicated expectations:

Tom expected to work hard, play hard, and buy a house. He never wanted children, but he did want to spend his life in a monogamous relationship with Brenda.

Brenda wanted to work hard and play hard. She also wanted to start a family about five years after marriage. That said, Brenda was bisexual, and expected that would "be cool" if she had a relationship with a woman from time to time.

Tom expected that once his career was settled, he could join another band and play professional gigs on the weekends without upsetting Brenda.

This example illustrates how unmet/uncommunicated expectations can linger for years and years. Like the prior example, these expectations had a negative impact on the couple's relationship. So, let's ask ourselves a similar set of questions:

Were any of these expectations unreasonable? If so, which ones?

When should Brenda and Tom have communicated their respective expectations in order to avoid conflict?

Now that the couple is 10 years into marriage and each has a set of unmet expectations, is there anything that can be done to fix the marriage or is it "too little, too late"?

*　*　*

Finally, we have Mark and Sonya. Sonya is the sole partner in her own law firm. She hired Mark four years ago to be her associate attorney. At the time, the firm was small and gave extensive attention to each client. Over the past four years, however, the firm's client list has grown substantially, and sometimes personal attention has to be sacrificed in order to get everything done. Here are some of Sonya and Mark's uncommunicated expectations:

Sonya always had plans to grow the firm as large as possible. She wanted a huge revenue stream while still delivering strong results. Mark, on the other hand, only joined the firm because he liked giving each client the attention he felt they deserved.

Mark expected a "work-life balance" when he joined Sonya's firm.

Sonya expected that both she and Mark would work whatever hours were necessary to grow the firm and its reputation.

Not surprisingly, Mark and Sonya began having serious disagreements four years into Mark's employment with the firm. In fact, at local networking events, Sonya began referring to Mark as "smart but unmotivated." In his interview with new potential employers, Mark labeled Sonya as a "slave-driver." Let's dive back in:

Were either Mark's or Sonya's expectations *unreasonable*? If so, how?

What would have happened if Mark and Sonya had each communicated their respective expectations during the time that Mark was interviewing for his job at Sonya's firm?

Is each "failed expectation" too big for the pair to work through?

Mark and Sonya each turned their unmet expectations into judgements of the other person. Was that fair? Would that have happened if the pair had communicated their expectations more clearly from the outset?

* * *

Of course, I ask all of these questions about all of these fictional people not because I expect you to fix their fictional problems. It's ok, Ms. Freud, they are make-believe—we don't have to fix them! I simply want you to see how many expectations we carry in life and how often we let those expectations go uncommunicated to the people we are closest to. I also want you to start thinking about the real-world impacts of uncommunicated and unreasonable expectations. I also want you to think about the harm that results when unmet expectations (whether those expectations were reasonable or not) turn into judgements.

So, now it's your turn. For purposes of this exercise, I want you to focus on one primary relationship in your life. It can be a relationship with a friend, significant other, or work colleague. Try to think about somebody who you feel has let you down recently—in other words, someone who has not met your expectations for the relationship. Ready to dive in? Let's go.

What unmet expectations are you currently experiencing with your person?

Do you feel like you have communicated those expectations fully and fairly? If so, how and when?

Have you ever considered that your expectations might be unreasonable? If so, how?

If you have not communicated your expectations to this person, how do you think your current relationship would differ had you taken the time to be honest and open about your expectations?

Do you think this other person has expectations from you that are currently unmet? If so, what are they?

Do you feel like those expectations were communicated to you sufficiently (both from a timing and substance perspective)? If not, how was the communication deficient?

Is there anything that you and this other person can do to meet each other's expectations going forward?

If not, discuss the incompatibility of your expectations.

If your expectations have gone unmet, did that cause you to transform your expectation into judgement? If so, how?

I don't care who you're thinking about, that exercise is *hard*. Let's explore why.

The self-interested vs. shared nature of expectations

Let me be clear about something. Many of the expectations we place on others in life are entirely selfish. We want *our* needs met, regardless of whether those needs completely align with the needs of others in our lives.

If, on the other hand, we communicate our expectations and align with people who are ok with those expectations, suddenly they become "shared expectations." And those, my friends, are a beautiful thing. Let me give you an example.

I have a friend, Jane, who was devastated when she learned that her husband, Patrick, didn't have any savings, despite the fact that he'd worked as a successful computer engineer for many years. Not only that, he had taken out several credit cards, maxed out every single one, and never made a single payment against the balances. Not surprisingly, she also learned at that time that Patrick had a gambling problem. All of these revelations led to extreme fights between the two and, eventually, to their divorce. Now, years after that split, Jane expects all of her future partners to be frugal, wealthy, and financially stable. Nonetheless, Jane has dated many people who are, by their very nature, quite the opposite.

They're not bad people. They don't lie about their financial situations like Patrick did. They just are who they are. They tend to be adventurous types who prioritize experiences and travel over large bank accounts. That said, if they want to be in a relationship with Jane, she *expects* them to be ultra financially savvy.

Think what you want about Jane and her experiences, but her expectation of financial stability is an issue of her own making. That sort of stability serves *her* needs in life. It may not serve her partners' needs. This also doesn't make Jane a bad person. It simply makes her someone who—if she wants her own needs to be met—needs to communicate this core expectation early and often in a relationship.

What I'm talking about here is *aligning* your expectations with the people who are important to you. If Jane is going to insist on financial stability, she needs to align herself with potential partners who share that expectation. With a shared expectation, the relationship can flourish. It's really that easy, except that's not easy at all.

None of us wants to start a new relationship (whether it is with a partner, friend, or colleague) by dredging out a giant list of our expectations. So, when do we have the conversation? Well, we can't even think about that until we've discussed the old cliché about "managing our expectations." As I told you before, I believe there is a healthy way to do this. And we're going to talk about it now.

Managing your expectations—the healthy way

Most of the time, when people talk of "managing expectations," they're referring to the sort of fatalistic thinking that comes from the folks I quoted at the outset of the chapter—you know, the "if you don't have expectations, you'll never be disappointed" crowd. They would have you bury *all* of your expectations in a simple quest to avoid disappointment.

As you know, I think that's bullshit.

Look, we're all going to have expectations. The way we "manage" them is not to ignore them, but to build a healthy relationship with them. And how do we do that? I propose a 4-step plan, which we'll break down below:

1. Honestly analyze for yourself whether your expectations in any given situation are reasonable.

2. Assuming you have a set of reasonable expectations, be prepared to prioritize them.

3. Ask yourself what it is going to feel like if your expectations are unmet.

4.   If you desire to, adjust your expectations so they align with the person you're assigning them to. If you don't want to adjust your expectations, think about adjusting the nature of the relationship.

Ok, let's talk about each step.

Are your expectations reasonable?

I am not proposing, of course, that you sit down and list every possible expectation in your life for an exhaustive review of reasonableness. If you did that, *my expectation* is that you'd keep yourself occupied for at least a decade.

What I am suggesting is that if you're faced with an expectation (or short list of expectations) that you think might impact an important relationship in your life, you need to really look at those expectations before you ever communicate them to the other person. In particular, you need to give yourself an honest analysis of whether those expectations are *reasonable*. Well, what the hell does that mean?

Reasonableness means different things to different people so I'm not going to sit here and try to define for you what is *and is not* reasonable. Once again, however, I am going to use an example to illustrate my point. Let's use the previous example of my friend Jane. Her issue with financial stability is frequently encountered within serious romantic relationships. This time, however, let's make this issue about YOU.

So, let's say you're in a relatively new relationship. It is your desire (and expectation) that your partner be financially responsible. Ok . . . at first blush, that doesn't seem too far-fetched. But for purposes of *this* analysis, you need to not only look at your own desires, but to also consider the other person, the status of your communications, and other factors that might impact reasonableness. For example, you might ask yourself:

How long have you been in a relationship with this person? If you've gone on one date and are expecting full disclosure on all things finance-related, that might be a tad less reasonable than if you've been dating for a couple of years.

Have you talked to this person about the issue of financial strategy? If so, what did you glean about the other person's feelings on the topic?

What do you know about the other person's history with finances? If this relationship started at a Debtor's Anonymous meeting, your expectation that he has unequivocal financial stability might be less reasonable than if you met in the waiting room of a financial analyst's office. Likewise, if your partner has revealed to you that they enjoyed unrestrained spending in the past, is it really reasonable for you to expect a sudden switch to financial perfection just to make you feel better?

You get the gist of the analysis, right? It all depends on the facts and circumstances you're faced with.

Whatever those are, I implore you to be honest with yourself not only about what you want and expect, but also about what the other person may truly want and expect.

Can you prioritize your reasonable expectations?

Ok, so you've done a little analysis and decided that your expectations are reasonable. In some instances, however, just because your expectations seem reasonable to you, does not mean they are all reasonable to the other person. In those cases, see if you can prioritize your expectations so that you and the other person can reach alignment.

Let's stick with financial stability as our theme. You've analyzed that expectation from both your perspective, as well as your partner's, and have determined that it seems reasonable. You realized during the analysis, however, that you have additional expectations related to financial stability. They might include things like:

Expecting that your partner puts 25% of his weekly paycheck into retirement savings;

Expecting that your partner maintain a credit score higher than 800; and

Expecting him to maintain a job that pays at least $150,000 per year.

Maybe each of those sub-expectations are reasonable (and maybe not). For purposes of this analysis, let's say that they are. Nonetheless, your partner has some conflicts with these expectations, namely:

While he routinely sets aside 20% of his paycheck for savings, he withdraws those savings annually so he can take an epic adventure trip each summer;

His current credit score remains tied in some respects to the spending habits of his ex-wife, and she was terribly irresponsible with money. Nonetheless, he has worked hard and has his credit score up to 730; and

While he has the skills and experience to earn $150,000 per year, he has chosen a job with a non-profit organization that pays roughly 80% of that sum.

None of those conflicts are inherently unreasonable, right? So, what can you do? Prioritize your expectations, of course!

For purposes of this illustration, the most important thing to Jane is that this person exhibits financial stability. In other words, that is her first priority. If retirement savings are also important, perhaps he can set aside a smaller percentage than what Jane expects while still taking excellent vacations each year. Conversely, Jane could increase the percentage of her income that is set aside for retirement. As for his credit score, Jane needs to decide whether the financial path he has walked since his marriage split up indicates that his credit score will eventually top her 800 point litmus test. And as for the salary? Come on . . . the guy is working for a non-profit that he really believes in. Can Jane drop the priority of that expectation so that she doesn't feel disappointed and he doesn't feel guilty?

The truth is, if we anticipate that our every expectation will be met in every instance, we are going to be sorely disappointed in life. If, on the other hand, we can prioritize those expectations that are *really* important to us, we're more likely to have healthy, happy relationships with others.

What if your expectations are unmet?

Thinking about this issue requires you to go back and revisit the first two prongs of this analysis. Let's say you've analyzed the expectation of financial stability from a partner and you find it to be both reasonable and of a high priority to you. You also believe (and can confirm—more on that later) that it is an expectation your partner can meet. That's an important belief because chances are, if that expectation goes unmet, you will be unhappy in the relationship. That's good to recognize very early on and we'll explore that below. For now, let's stick to the "simpler" expectations.

Specifically, what if those sub-expectations are unmet? What if, one Saturday, your partner decides to purchase a vintage car that he has always wanted instead of putting a percentage of his salary into savings that month? Is that going to cause you to flip out, or can you handle it? (Might I suggest that if that *is* going to make you flip out, you consider your own control issues).

But I digress . . .

My point is, if you're not going to be able to handle any unmet expectations, you need to be honest with yourself (and your partner) about that early on. When you do that, you have the ability to adjust your respective needs, wants, and expectations so no one has an unreasonable reaction. And, as noted, that will probably be easier to do with expectations to which you've assigned a lower priority.

To adjust, or not to adjust?

Alright, so let's take this one step further. This time let's assume you've decided (after thorough analysis) that your partner cannot and will not meet your primary expectation of maintaining habits that lead to financial stability. You have a couple of options here—you always have options in life, whether or not you like them is another thing. In this instance, you probably won't like them so I'm just going to be blunt about it.

You can:

Decide that this person's place in your life is more important than your need for his financial prowess (and adjust your expectation accordingly); or

You can walk away before somebody gets hurt, knowing that if *this* expectation goes unmet, the relationship will not survive.

The good news is, this decision is entirely up to you. You *own* your expectations and you are entitled to respect them. The bad news is, either of the above decisions will be *hard*. Nonetheless, those are your options . . . unless you have a better plan, in which case, I'd like to hear it.

Whatever you do, remember that it is not fair to you or your partner for you to turn your unmet expectations into judgements.

I can almost hear your skepticism in my head: "Okay genius, so when does all this communication happen?" Very fair question.

If you are anything like the friends and colleagues I talked to while I wrote this book, you may totally buy into the concept of expectations, yet still believe that there is no good time to have a conversation about them. That's fair. After all, very few of us have been brought up to talk about this stuff, or even to process it for ourselves.

In other words, we are almost chartering unknown territory on this issue. As a result, all I can give you is anecdotal evidence, along with my own rather strong opinion. Are you ready for this? Here's my grand advice on precisely when you should begin talking to another person about your expectations:

When it feels right.

We've already talked about how you need to be reasonable in having these conversations. I assume you've digested that. The simple truth is that there will come a time in many relationships when you feel like it is time to move the relationship forward. That's the time when you should start doing your analysis of expectations.

And once you've decided your expectations are reasonable, you've set your priorities, and you've created clear boundaries for yourself regarding how much you're willing to adjust—well then, what's stopping you?

If you don't believe me, go back and look at your failed relationships. Could they have benefited from this type of discussion? If so, when do you think it would have been an appropriate time to discuss them? If you had done that, do you think the relationship would have been different? If so, how?

I'm not kidding around here. I really want you to think about this stuff. It may not save the relationships you've already let go of, but it just may give you the clarity you need in all the relationships you have going forward. Well, with one caveat, that is . . .

What does the other person expect?

You know what I'm going to say here, right? Everything is not all about you all the time. Just as you have expectations for your relationships, the other people in your life have their own expectations. So, if you're going to become an active advocate of expectations, you better be ready for the people in your life to speak up about their needs too.

How do you deal with that? Well, for one thing, you can analyze their expectations the same way you've analyzed yours:

Are their expectations reasonable?

If so, do they need to be prioritized in a way that will make you or the other person more comfortable?

How will the other person feel if their core expectations are unmet?

And finally, if you decide their expectation is valid—even if it is outside your comfort zone—can you adjust your needs and expectations so that you align with the other person while still remaining authentically you?

These may be easy steps to recite but the analysis is actually very hard. Yet, isn't a great relationship worth the effort? Imagine being able to be authentically you while supporting someone else being authentically them!

What could be better?

Maybe nothing—but understand that this process will require you to be incredibly vulnerable. After all, you're opening yourself up with respect to boundaries, needs, wants, and desires—not all of which may be part of popular culture. And at this point, the other person is doing the same thing. As I said, it won't be easy. But if you both can receive communication without casting judgement, you may just find something that is incredibly special.

One last anecdote

As you now know, I talked to a lot of people as I formed this chapter. One conversation in particular struck me so much that I wanted to end this chapter with the lesson that resulted.

Here we go:

I was speaking to my friend Matthew, who happens to have a host of mental health challenges, including anxiety, severe depression, and obsessive-compulsive disorder. You'll never meet a nicer guy or a better friend. Nonetheless, Matthew has difficulty letting go of painful thoughts or anxiety-producing situations.

Almost as long as I've known this guy, he has had trouble with his elderly father. As he explained it to me, his father was physically and emotionally abusive to Matthew during his youth. Meanwhile, the father was always exceptionally favorable to (and uncritical of) Matthew's sister, Judy.

By the time Matthew and I had the subject conversation, he hadn't spoken to his father in over three years. He was reeling because he had written a letter to his father some five months ago and had never received a response.

For weeks on end, I listened to Matthew go on and on about his disappointment with his father's unresponsiveness. Then I started writing this chapter and decided to have a frank conversation with my friend. And, trust me, I had tried to have frank conversations with Matthew on this topic previously. Each time, I was met with an outright objection to any notion other than that his father was an unfathomable asshole. This conversation, however, was different.

First, I explained my recent work on this chapter to Matthew. Then I popped the question:

"Matthew," I said, "what if the issue isn't that your dad is an asshole? What if you're expecting him to act like a normal dad when clearly—given your abusive upbringing—he is not? Could it be that you continue to hurt yourself by setting your expectations too high for someone who is not capable of ever joining you where you need him to be?"

Matthew paused for a long while. At least a minute. I could tell his mind was churning.

"Hmmmm . . . " he said. "You may be onto something. I do keep expecting him to act like a normal dad, yet everything in my life has told me he is not that. Maybe I do need to adjust my expectations."

I, of course, was patting myself on the back as Matthew reached his revelation. At the same time, I knew I was really doing groundbreaking work. Matthew's expectations of his father were entirely unreasonable. Were they reasonable for a "normal" dad? Sure! But his dad was anything but that.

For the next two hours, Matthew and I dissected this notion and eventually, he gave up on the idea that he would ever get the comfort he needed from his dad. Then, we talked about the grief he'd have to deal with in letting go of those unreasonable and unmet expectations.

Today, my dear friend is processing this grief with a therapist. That said, he is no longer chained to the idea that he can expect reasonable behavior from his dad. He's let that go and says he is much better for it. I couldn't be happier for him.

While Matthew's example is an extreme one, it is also entirely instructive. And I want you to think about it in the context of your own life and your own expectations. Is there someone you've been expecting something from who simply cannot give it to you? If so, is it time to let go of those expectations and come to peace with who they are (even if you have to move on)?

When it comes to expectations, I think all of us have some learning and growing to do. Are you willing to do that with me now? If you are not willing to go there now, you'll be at a disadvantage in all the other chapters.

"Here's to the crazy ones.
The misfits. The rebels. The troublemakers.
The round pegs in the square holes.
The ones who see things differently.
They're not fond of rules.
And they have no respect
for the status quo.
You can quote them, disagree with them,
glorify or vilify them.
About the only thing you can't do
is ignore them.
Because they change things.
They push the human race forward.
While some may see them
as the crazy ones,
we see genius.
Because the people
who are crazy enough to think
they can change the world,
are the ones who do."
—Apple Commercial, 1997

Three

Cultural Confines

Before babies are even born onto this planet, culture starts sending them messages. Don't believe me? Take a moment and search for a "gender reveal" party on the internet. Chances are, you'll come up with endless videos of anxious couples doing any assortment of antics to inform the world about the sex of their baby, still *in utero*. Cut into a cake and find a pink center? It's a girl! Pop a balloon only to be showered with blue confetti? Congratulations! It's a boy! And so, it begins . . .

From that moment on, society bombards us with messages about how we're "supposed" to be. Of course, much of the messaging continues to be about gender. Those pink-dress wearing girls are all "sugar and spice and everything nice," right? And the boys? Well, "snips and snails and puppy dog tails"—*that* is apparently what little boys are made of. As the little one grows, girls will be gifted with dolls and stuffed animals and frilly dresses. Boys will get toy trucks and trains and fireman gear. Because, well, that's what our culture expects.

As we grow older, the cultural messages continue. Women's magazines are mostly about fashion and gossip and how to catch a man. Men's' magazines are about sports and unattached sex and business things. But the cultural confines don't stop with gender.

Have you ever considered phrases like "black hat tactics," "blackballed," "blacklisted," "black sheep," "black out," "black magic," or "black death"? If you don't think those create a cultural association between "bad" and all things black (including people), you're sorely mistaken. If you don't believe me on that, go talk to people of color about the topic.

Or, have you ever wondered why school books continue to teach false narratives (e.g., "Columbus discovered America! What a hero! Let's celebrate Columbus Day!") or why movies continue to be made that enforce old stereotypes (for example, read "9 Harmful Stereotypes We Never Realized Our Favorite Disney Movies Taught Us")*.

To make matters worse, we also get these messages from the people closest to us. Consider these examples:

From parents:
"That is not the way a lady behaves!"
"Boys don't cry."
"Act like a big boy/girl!"
"Don't be so sensitive."
"Someday you'll be the man of the house."
"Because I'm the mom and I said so, that's why."

From teachers:
"Girls do not play football at recess."
"Act your age."
"Maybe you're just not a math person."
"Everybody else is able to do it, why can't you?"
"Don't do that—it's against the rules!"

From friends:
"What's your problem? Everybody's doing it!"
"One sip isn't going to kill you."
"Did you see how fat [random female pop star] has gotten?"
"If you like her, you should just ignore her for a while."
"Don't be such a fag. Just do it!"

While some of these statements are obviously problematic, others just seem to be part of the status quo—part of our culture. And for

---

* 9 Harmful Stereotypes We Never Realized Our Favorite Disney Movies Taught Us, April 25, 2014, by Michelle Juergen and found at: https://www.mic.com/articles/88167/9-harmful-stereotypes-we-never-realized-our-favorite-disney-movies-taught-us

many people, that's ok. We're presented with—and expected to accept—thousands of "norms" in our lifetimes. For most people, that's enough.

But what if it's not enough for you? What if the status quo doesn't make any sense whatsoever to you? I'm here to tell you that *that* is ok too. You don't have to live by any of the cultural confines that have been forced down your throat for all these years.

That said, there are both good ways and bad ways to deal with this (and, yes, I'm fully aware of how "judgy" the terms good and bad are). Here is my recipe for questioning, and sometimes rejecting, those cultural confines. It happens in three parts. And, in case you don't think I really believe in this three-pronged test, I should tell you that I taught it to my two daughters from a very young age and I am immensely proud of how they've lived out these strategies in their everyday lives. Here are the steps I suggest you take any time you are questioning a cultural confine:

1. Feel free to question everything (especially when you're not "supposed to").

2. Be respectful.

3. Be prepared to suffer the consequences of your questioning.

Let's break each step down so you can see what I'm talking about.

Question everything

Have you ever been in a structured situation (let's say a classroom, church, or work meeting) and thought to yourself "What the f* are these people talking about? This is crazy!" Did you say that out loud or did you just think it? If you're like most people, you just thought it, and moved on with your life.

Or maybe you mentioned your indignance to someone else later in the day. If so, I bet you were met with responses like:

"I get it. That's just the way people are."

"Well, sure . . . but it's not our job to question this."

"The Lord works in mysterious ways."

"Those are the rules."

Did you accept that bullshit? For me, responses like that are infuriating. In fact, they are the antithesis of progress. And history proves this point. For example, what if, when asked to give up her seat on the bus for a white man, Rosa Parks simply accepted the status quo, got up, and said to herself, "oh well, those are the rules." What a tragedy!

Instead, she questioned the cultural confine and, in refusing to give up her seat, changed the course of history. Indeed, on that day, with one simple act, she came to be known as the "mother of the civil rights movement." What's your legacy going to be?

Or consider Sandra Day O'Connor, the first female Justice on the United States Supreme Court. Justice O'Connor attended Stanford Law School. When she graduated in 1952, she was among the top 10% of her class. So, to recap . . . she graduated from one of the very best law schools in the country and her grades placed her among the top scholars from her graduating class. Her classmates (almost exclusively men) were immediately hired by some of the most prestigious law firms and government agencies in the country.

As for O'Connor? She was only offered jobs as a legal secretary. Why? Well, because the cultural confines of the time dictated that women couldn't or shouldn't work as lawyers. Justice O'Connor could have accepted that. She could have taken a job as a secretary, despite all her hard work, and that would have been that.

Instead, she offered to work as a deputy attorney for a small county in California *for absolutely no pay*. There, she proved her worth (though she was still forced to sit with the secretarial pool). She was eventually granted a small salary—far lower than those provided to her male colleagues—and could call herself a working attorney.

Despite her ridiculous wages, she put her head down and continued to work. That was her form of protest. And, by 1965, she was the Attorney General for the State of Arizona. In 1981, she was appointed to the United States Supreme Court.

Like Rosa Parks, O'Connor's persistence and insistence on questioning the status quo changed the course of history. Today, according to some sources, women make up 60% of America's attorneys. (Of course, how those women are paid compared to men is another story . . .)

My point in telling you about these two women is this—these are two individuals who questioned everything around them. Even though millions of their contemporaries just accepted the status quo (or the *cultural confines* for POC and women), they did not.

They questioned why they couldn't do the things that other people could. And thank goodness they did. They also did so in a way that aligns with my other two strategies for questioning those cultural confines. So, let's move on to those, shall we?

Be respectful

Here's where a lot of people who question the status quo go off course—they're jerks about it. They whine or complain or throw temper tantrums. And, resultantly, they're often ignored, ridiculed, and rejected by the very people whose minds they aim to change. An effective strategy? Probably not. But just because their methods are off-course doesn't mean their questions aren't appropriate. The key to successful challenges to the status quo is to be respectful.

Let's go back to Rosa Parks. She didn't climb on the bus that day screaming and yelling. Contrary to what most people believe, she didn't even take a seat in the front of the bus. Rather, she sat in the first row of the "Colored Section."

The bus was crowded that day, however, and when the "White Section" filled, Ms. Parks and three others were asked to give up their seats for white passengers. While the other three complied, Rosa Parks politely refused. Her protest was respectful.

Years later, she wrote in her autobiography, "People always say that I didn't give up my seat because I was tired but that isn't true. I was not tired physically . . . No, the only tired I was, was tired of giving in." In other words, she was tired of the cultural confines. And she chose a polite, respectful way of expressing that.

As for Justice O'Connor, she could have done a lot of things differently with her resistance to the status quo as well. She could have sued the employers who only offered her secretarial jobs. She could have flattened somebody's tires or keyed somebody's car (I would have been tempted). Instead, she pounded on doors, offering to work as a highly qualified lawyer for free, until someone said yes. She knew the cultural confine that prohibited her from practicing as an attorney was wrong, and she chose a respectful (and ultimately, successful) way of challenging it.

Think about the cultural confines that you are questioning in your own life. Are you mad about them? Good, you should be. Take a minute and think about all the rageful things you could do to protest that state of affairs. It's fun to think about isn't it? But now, I want you to take *three* minutes and think about all of the respectful ways you could launch your protest.

Which do you think would be more conducive to the actual change you seek? Let's use a real-world example:

Let's say you're a present-day female attorney. You're married to a wonderful man who is an accountant. The two of you have three children, aged three, five, and seven. Because your kids are all in different stages of their schooling (pre-school, kindergarten, and grammar school), there are multiple drop-off and pick-up times to maneuver. Additionally, your family has to take care of the basics like cooking, shopping, laundry, house-cleaning, and yard care. Let's also say that in the natural course of things, you have become the person responsible for all of those household duties, except yard care. Your husband takes care of that each Saturday.

I work with a lot of professionals in my coaching business and I can tell you, this is not an unusual scenario. And, of course, it largely stems from decades of cultural confines saying that women are responsible for most of the cooking, cleaning, and childcare within a family. Notwithstanding the fact that women make up 50% of the modern workforce, this state of affairs is shockingly common (though no less shocking).

So, you find yourself in this situation and you want to question the validity of your arrangement. Let's take a look at the two choices for protest that we talked about above: rage and respect. If you choose rage, what are your options? You could leave your husband, abandon your kids, and find an easy-to-maintain studio apartment somewhere. You could also yell at your husband constantly, be short-tempered with your children, and drink a lot after everyone else has gone to bed and nobody's watching you. Those are all strategies that might ultimately change your situation.

Or, you could react with respect. You could sit your husband down for a calm, well-planned discussion where you offer him the option of helping more or agreeing that your family needs to pay for outside help.

You could be honest about your fatigue, helplessness, and growing sense of resentment. Or perhaps you could silently just stop performing all of the household chores (save for those that keep your kids alive, of course) and see if he gets the message. Either way, you're likely to get a much better result by being respectful in your approach. You may not change the world (not every act of protest does) but you might just change *your world*. And sometimes that is enough.

Be prepared for the consequences

Of course, regardless of whether your protest is rageful or respectful, consequences are sure to follow. Rosa Parks, for example, was arrested by two police officers before the bus ever moved from the spot where she refused to give up her seat. Sandra Day O'Connor worked her ass off in law school only to have to work for no pay. In other words, both had consequences stemming from their acts of protest.

And that's ok, isn't it? All of our actions have consequences. If we exercise, we lose weight. If we rob a grocery store, we go to jail. If we enter into a profession that has historically rejected people like us, we find it hard to get a job. That's life.

The problem is, too many people forget to really consider the consequences before they act out in protest of the status quo. Take the example of our modern-day attorney, above. The ultimate consequences of her rageful reactions might be isolation, loneliness, or a bad legal position in her eventual divorce. The consequences of her respectful reactions might be the same but would more likely fall along the lines of a better relationship with her husband, relief from all that housework, or, at the very least, a girls' weekend every once in a while.

Obviously, I'm not advocating that you decide to take action only if the consequences are minimal. To the contrary, I want you to question the cultural confines that hold you down. I want you to do so even if the consequences will be severe! I simply ask that you consider them before you act. And, consider whether they are consequences you can live with. Not all of them are. And that's ok too.

I want to tell you about an amazing moment when my youngest daughter, Sydney—during junior high school, mind you—went through this precise process (much to my delight). She questioned the norm, acted respectfully in her response, and made a conscious decision to accept the consequences of her actions. Here's how it went down:

One day, I got a call from the principal. He was calling to inform me that my daughter had been caught skipping her PE class. She had been "caught" in the girls locker room when she should have been out on the field. I thought to myself, "wow, that was a tough case to break, Principal, you must have had to bring out the hound dogs to find her." But I kept listening, especially since that didn't sound like my kid at all. PE was her favorite class, for shit's sake.

"Was she doing drugs?" I asked.

"No," he said.

"Was she making out with a boy?"

Again, "No."

"Was she defacing public property?"

"Was she being disrespectful?"

"Did she push a little old lady down?"

"No", "No", "No."

"Why are you calling me? Did you ask Syd why she spent her PE class time in the locker room?"

His response was something along the lines of "mutter, mutter, I don't know." I immediately wondered who put him in charge.

When I got a chance to talk to Syd later, I learned the following. The PE teacher was notoriously mean (I knew this prior to the day in question). That day, the class was supposed to be graded on a series of drills. One of the girls in the class was not a very skilled athlete. As a matter of fact, PE was her worst nightmare only to be made worse by a PE teacher who probably pulled the wings off of flies for fun. The PE teacher had made fun of the little girl ruthlessly in the past and made her feel completely inadequate. On that day, the girl was filled with anxiety, and terrified to do drills (for which she would be ridiculed) in front of everyone.

Syd saw the girl crying and overtaken with fear in the locker room. At that moment, Syd made the conscious decision to stay there with her in a back area of the locker room until all the kids had exited out on the field. Syd consoled her and helped her pass the time so she didn't have to be bullied yet again by a PE teacher who was intoxicated with power.

When I heard that explanation, I couldn't have been more proud. Syd even reminded me that I had taught her to think for herself and to also always consider the consequences of her actions. She told me unapologetically that she had known she would get in trouble but that taking a stand against the bullying teacher was more important to her than those consequences. She accepted the ramifications of skipping class like a champ. Syd chose to buck the system that day and I could not have been happier about it.

I was, however, livid with the school for its failure of leadership. But that's a story for another day.

So, with that story in mind, now is a good time for you to think about any consequences you have faced in life that—had you thought of them in advance—would have changed your course of action. Maybe you decided to make an inattentive boyfriend jealous by flirting with one of his friends, only to find that your actions caused him to dump you rather than to pay more attention to you. Or maybe you decided not to give a lot of effort in a class required for your major—only to wind up with a failing grade and an inability to graduate on time.

On the other hand, maybe you've been surprised by positive consequences. Let's say you protested your workload in the office only to be met with a new assistant the following week. Or perhaps you set a boundary within your relationship only to find your partner was more than willing to comply—resulting in a happier, healthier union. Those things can definitely happen too. So, what's your story?

At this point, I want you to create a journal entry. Write about a time that you were dissatisfied with the status quo. Write about how you questioned or challenged that cultural confine and then, of course, write about the consequences of your actions.

If the consequences were less than ideal, ask yourself these questions:

Was I respectful in my questioning of that cultural confine? If not, how could I have made my questioning more respectful? Would that have changed the outcome?

Did I consider the consequences before I acted? If not, how would my consideration of the consequences have changed the outcome?

After you've completed that exercise, sit with your journal entry for a while. Let it sink in. Be honest with yourself about your responsibility for any negative outcomes that resulted from your actions.

Now, I want you to think about a cultural confine that currently baffles you. Remember, it doesn't have to be a life-changer or a situation that impacts everyone in the world. It can be, but it can also be highly personal (like why I have to take a math class in order to get my degree in English?) Get out your pen and paper again because you're going to make another journal entry.

If there is a status quo you seek to challenge, write it down. This time, however, write about how you can challenge it with respect.

Who can you talk to about it?

What form of non-violent, simple protest might effectuate change?

Who else might join your cause?

Will they sign on to act respectfully in pursuit of change?

Once you've considered those questions, I want you to take a deep dive into all the possible consequences—good and bad. If you come up with negative consequences, ask yourself whether taking the proposed action is worth those consequences. If not, consider whether a different action in protest of the same condition might get you a better result. Or conversely, write about why a negative consequence is acceptable.

Rosa Parks, for example, probably wasn't shocked by her arrest. But that negative consequence sparked a revolution so, for her, it was likely worth it in the long run.

Take your time and really explore these questions. There's no reason why any of us has to live a life without questioning cultural "norms" that are not acceptable to us. And, best of all, we all have the ability to make rational decisions, led by respect and consideration of consequences, to change anything.

"I do not feel obliged to believe that the same God who has endowed us with sense, reason, and intellect has intended for us to forgo their use."

—Galileo

Four

Religion

Let me be clear from the outset: the purpose of this chapter is not to bash religion. Or to tell you to abandon it. Or even to recruit you from one sect to another. No, the purpose of this chapter is simply to discuss the impact religion may (or may not) have on our lives, and to develop strategies for questioning doctrines that might keep us from living our most authentic lives.

Even if I wanted to pull you away from your belief system, I seriously doubt that I could. Look, religion has existed, in one form or another, since the dawn of humanity. And while the names of the Gods and the detailed rules may vary among the myriad of religions that exist today, most share many of the same core tenants (we'll talk about some of those, below).

Consequently, we'll also explore strategies for aligning ourselves with religious doctrines that *do* foster our authentic selves, even if we have to let go of much of the rest of it. So, sit back, relax, and let's have a frank discussion about religion.

What's so great about religion?

The answer to this question is easy, actually. There's a *lot* that is great about religion. Community. Order. Fellowship. Guidelines. Love. Celebration. Ritual. And that's all just off the top of my head. But nonetheless, it's worth breaking down.

Where else can you go every week, without fail, and know that you're going to find dozens (if not hundreds) of like-minded people who are there for the same reason as you? How often do you find a group of that size who wants to study the same book (or the same philosophy) as intently as you do? What other institution provides you with an endless supply of free lectures, classes, study groups, and opportunities for learning? Not only that, but most of these places also offer free, unending counseling services with a trained professional who cares deeply for your well-being. When you break it down this way, church sounds pretty great.

And we haven't even begun to discuss the order, rules, and guidelines that religions offer. Are you the type of person who needs structure and who unflinchingly follows the rules? Religion may be just the thing for you. Most religions supply us with an endless set of regulations on everything from who we should marry (and when) to how our families should grieve when we die. For many people, these rules quell some of the major anxieties that can arise when we simply don't know what to do with all the options presented to us in this life.

Oh, I'm not done yet, Mother Mary. How about the singing and chanting? Where else do we get to go, as adults, where we're not just encouraged—but actually *expected*—to sing at the top of our lungs? In fact, these days, churches are the favored venue among would-be rock stars and other musicians who don't have access to public gigs elsewhere. I'm not knocking those folks. I actually think it's great that modern churches have moved from the pipe organ to the electric guitar.

Yes, there is so much that is great about religion—*and we haven't even talked about God yet.* Step away from your personal, preconceived notions of religion for a moment and think about how amazing the concept of God is. There is an all-knowing, all-seeing, compassionate, loving, generous being in the sky who is *always* available to listen to your problems. You can *always* ask him/her/it for guidance. You can ask for favors. You can seek solace. You can admit your deepest, darkest secrets. You can disclose your fears and your desires. You can ask for forgiveness.

And this being, this God, won't tell anyone what you've revealed. Moreover, if you're a true believer, you also count on this entity to actually solve (or help you solve) all of your woes. Just thinking about it makes me want to get on my knees and pray. Then I want to get up and run to my nearest church to fill out a membership application.

That's a thing, right?

Although my tone is joking, I'm rather serious. All of these things are *wonderful* aspects of religion. And they have kept people satisfied, complacent, happy, and relatively ordered for centuries. So, what's the problem? You didn't think I was just going to give religion a complete pass, did you?

What's the problem with religion?

I honestly don't think there is one overall *problem* with religion. Sure, I could point to various scandals, wars, acts of oppression, and other egregious happenings perpetrated in the name of religion. But I'm not going to. I want to talk about how religion can negatively impact us on a much more personal level.

Remember those rules we talked about just a bit ago? Well, I maintain that they can be a good thing for a lot of people. That said, many of those rules were written thousands of years ago and "may" not be the healthiest rules for modern humans—and women in particular.

This is true even though a 2014 Pew Research Center study revealed that women are more likely than men (60% vs. 47%) to say religion is "very important" in their lives and are more likely than men to attend weekly religious services (40% vs. 32%).

And sometimes, that is what confounds me. Modern women seem to flock to religion more fervently than men, even while many religious teachings and rules historically aim to hold them down.

Let's take a brief look at some of the rules and principles I'm talking about—and, keep in mind, these come from *only two* of the major religions in the world:

"A woman should learn in quietness and full submission. I do not permit a woman to teach or to have authority over a man. She must be silent." 1 Timothy 2:11-15.

"And they ask you about menstruation. Say, 'It is harm, so keep away from wives during menstruation. And do not approach them until they are pure . . . '" Quran 2:222.

"Wives, submit to your husbands, as is fitting to the Lord." Colossians 3:18.

"Men are in charge of women by [right of] what Allah has given one over the other and what they spend [for maintenance] from their wealth. So righteous women are devoutly obedient, guarding in [the husband's] absence what Allah would have them guard. But those [wives] from whom you fear arrogance— [first] advise them; [then if they persist], forsake them in bed; and [finally], strike them." Quran 4:34.

"Now I want you to realize that the head of every man is Christ, and the head of the woman is man." 1 Corinthians 11:3-16.

"And bring to witness two witnesses from among your men. And if there are not two men [available], then a man and two women from those whom you accept as witnesses—so that if one of the women errs, then the other can remind her . . . " Quran 2:282.

I could literally go on for centuries—because religion has. And please understand that I am not intending to zero in on Christianity and Islam and suggest that they are better or worse than any of the others. This isn't a treatise on comparative religion—I was simply trying to make a point using the two religions that collectively make up over 50% of all believers around the globe.

The truth is, outside of a handful of women-centric belief systems (many of which all but disappeared along with the rise of Christianity), religion has often been used as a tool to, among many other things, keep women in a very narrow lane within our society.

Wife, mother, nun, helper. What else?

And yes, I recognize that most modern churches are not terribly strict with these rules. But they do exist, and they do inform our decisions and our behavior. Sadly, they are also often used to justify bad behavior on the part of men within the church. Have you experienced this? Many of us have, me included.

Regardless of whether your experiences with religion have been good or bad, I want you to stop right now and write down the ways that religion has impacted your status as a woman in this world. Even if you weren't brought up in a religious household or have never made religion a major part of your life—I'm guessing it has impacted you. Here are some questions to stimulate your thinking on the topic:

1. Which religion have you been exposed to the most in life?

2. Have you ever felt like you were treated differently than others based on religious doctrine?

   a. When did that first happen?

   b. How were you treated differently?

3. Does your religion put any particular restrictions on women (the way you dress, for example)?

4. How do you feel about the way your religion treats women?

5. Has your religion's treatment of women ever impacted the decisions you've made in life? If so, how?

6. Have you ever disagreed with a particular doctrine taught by your religion?

7. Have you ever agreed with a doctrine that other people believe hold women down?

8. Have you ever felt conflicted by your love for your religion and some of its rules that negatively impact women?

Authentic living within the confines of religion

It's quite possible that the above exercise left you feeling very confident about your relationship with your religion. If so, that's awesome. If, on the other hand, you recognized that there are some gaps in your comfort with religion, I understand. It's ok. It doesn't mean you have to throw away your religion and it doesn't mean you have to throw away your authenticity. It just means you have to marry the two.

One of the easiest ways to do this is to study some of the fundamental teachings that are shared by most of the major religions—ideas that I think we can all agree are beautiful, life-fulfilling principles to live by.

Many people have done this, but for purposes of researching this chapter, I've focused on similarities identified by the Integral Church—a group made up of philosophers and writers like Friedrich Nietzsche, Rudolf Steiner, Sri Aurobindo, and Aldous Huxley, just to name a few.

According to them, the world's great religions all teach the following in one form or another:

Blessed Are the Peacemakers—When people live in the awareness that there is a close kinship between all individuals and nations, peace is the natural result.

Heaven is Within—The power and love of God is available within each of us. Example: "Even as the scent dwells within the flower, so God within thine own heart forever abides."—Sikhism

People Do Not Live by Bread Alone—The blessings of life are deeper than what can be appreciated by the senses.

Be Slow to Anger—Anger clouds the mind in the very moments that clarity and objectivity are needed most. Example: "He who holds back rising anger like a rolling chariot, him I call a real driver; others only hold the reins."—Buddha

Love Thy Neighbor / Conquer With Love / All You Need is Love—Acts of faith, prayer, and deep meditation provide us with the strength that allows love for our fellow humans to become an abiding part of our lives. Love is a unifying force.

Indeed, if you do take the time to study comparative religion, you will undoubtedly see that themes of love, compassion, peace, gratitude, and kindness resonate throughout most of the guiding texts. For purposes of this chapter, let's call these ideals the "Core Beliefs," shall we?

As a starting place for living our authentic lives within religion—even if some of the more detailed rules feel confining to us—what if we chose to focus our spiritual practice on the Core Beliefs?

I don't care who you are or what your predominant religious practice is, I honestly think every single one of us would benefit from making these universal themes more central to our lives. And, if we can truly incorporate the Core Beliefs into our lives, we give ourselves a peaceful platform from which to start questioning the things that bother us about our own religion. So, how the heck do we do that?

To begin with, you already know that there is a whole additional chapter in this book dealing with the *other* cultural confines—you just read it. That chapter discusses things like media, family, culture, generation, etc. As you hopefully recall, I gave a detailed analysis for challenging those cultural norms that you believe hold you down in life. It would be incredibly redundant for me to repeat that analytical procedure here. Therefore, if it has been a while since you picked up this book, you might want to go back and familiarize yourself with those concepts.

Are you ready? Great, let's move on and focus on the three main steps for challenging any cultural confine. Here, of course, we'll focus solely on religion.

Questioning

Look, there's not a chance that any of us will agree 100% with every single thing our religion teaches us. And guess what? That's ok. The first step in getting around those rules, however, is to intelligently question them.

In my days as a young angelic child, I (of course) had my own way of questioning. Albeit not very sophisticated, I did get my point across. I had been through all of the catechism classes and preparation that the Catholic Church requires to receive my first sacrament of penance. For the non-Catholics in the room, that meant I had to learn how to go and tell on myself (confess) to a priest so that he could give me some prayers to say (penance) and then I would be good to go again (because he absolved me of my wrong doings).

I knew there was this thing called a confessional and that somehow it made confession easier if you were incognito or anonymous. In my thinking, since I was going to be laying out all my sins as a 12 year old, we (the priest and I) needed to have an in depth discussion.

I showed up for my first confession on Saturday afternoon and waited in line to speak with the big guy. I was rehearsing my list over and over in my head so as not to forget anything. My palms began to sweat as I was "next." The door creaked open, the person that was in there hung their head and walked into the church. The door shut behind them.

Now, you should know, I went to a church that was newer in its construction. So, the powers that engineered this cone of secrecy put the priest's office right off of the confessional. As my big moment arrived, I went right around the confessional, opened the priest's office door and walked straight in and confidently planted myself on his couch.

First off, the couch was a helluva lot more comfy than kneeling on wood and if I am going to bear my soul, I wanted to have some sort of relationship with the person who was going to hear all my secrets. To say the priest was shocked would be an understatement. He politely offered for me to go try again and this time make it into the confessional. And I politely declined. It didn't make sense for me.

I confessed, he gave me my penance, but every time after that, he knew who I was. I got you Father—me and you! Our bond was all in my head, but it made me feel better.

When I shared my story with my friend Jennifer, she also recalled an early experience with defying the constraints of religion.

Jennifer was around seven years old and was sitting in Sunday school which, for a variety of reasons, she hated. On that particular Sunday, her teacher was explaining to the class that anyone who dies without "asking for forgiveness for their sins" would go to hell (which was explained with all the fire and brimstone you can imagine). One of the other kids raised their hand and asked, "what if a baby dies right after it is born? It can't even think yet to ask for forgiveness. Will it go to hell?"

Within only the slightest of pauses, Jennifer's Sunday school teacher sighed and said, "Sadly, yes."

Well, this was too much for her young spirit to take. What kind of God would send a baby into eternal hellfire for something it had no control over? Jennifer remembers her little-kid brain getting madder and madder as the hour progressed.

When she finally met her mom at the car after the class had ended, she promptly announced that she was never going back to Sunday school because, as she perceived it, "God hates babies."

Now, I applaud Jennifer for taking a stance against a rule that her particular church advocated and that she could not tolerate. Of course, being seven, she did not get to leave the church—her mom wasn't having any of that. But, as she describes it, that was the day that she stopped paying attention. And actually, that's a little sad.

Had Jennifer been older and wiser, she could have questioned her church's interpretation of that rule. She could have met with the pastor and discussed it. She could have truly analyzed how strongly she wanted to be associated with that church when its teachings were so contrary to her soul. And, she could have studied other religious teachings that could have tempered her anger.

A quote from Hinduism comes to mind here:

"Study the words, no doubt, but look behind them to the thought they indicate; And having found it, throw the words away, as chaff when you have sifted out the grain."

That's a beautiful sentiment and I think it is incredibly important for any of us who question certain tenets of our religion. Maybe, just maybe, we don't have to take our religious texts so literally. Maybe, for example, Jennifer could have looked at the sentiment behind what her Sunday school teacher was trying to convey, which was simply, "In our religion, one must be forgiven in order to enter heaven." It's possible Jennifer could have worked with or worked around that philosophy.

The point is this: Questions are ok. Just make sure they are well thought out. Think about the ways that the rule you're questioning could be altered to align with your authentic self.

Then, ask yourself whether that alignment is possible and healthy. And, of course, it never hurts to get counsel from your pastor, rabbi, preacher, etc., as you ponder these thoughts.

The only thing I ask that you *not* do is stuff down your questions and live your life as if everything was perfect. That's a good recipe for heartache, poor health, and ever-growing discontent.

Be respectful during the process

From what I understand, Jennifer's seven-year-old self was not terribly subtle about her discontent with Sunday school. I'm pretty sure she was rude to the teacher that fateful day and she tells me she likely sat with her arms crossed and a scowl on her face for as long as that teacher was in charge of that class. But whatever . . . she was seven.

As adults, we have better communication tools to work with. And unless you are in the strictest of modern churches, I'm willing to bet that the head of your church will welcome your thoughtful questions. In fact, I'm guessing that even the pastor of a church you don't belong to would entertain your questions so long as you were respectful.

I know you've already read about this in the chapter on cultural confines, so I won't belabor the point. Just remember that your respect of religion will go a long way toward having your questions answered with thought and introspection.

Be prepared for the consequences

Again, having read the chapter on cultural confines, you undoubtedly know that I advocate a thorough analysis of possible consequences before you "buck the system," so to speak. When it comes to religion, however, I want you to be exceptionally cognizant of this part of the equation.

For example, what if the answers you're seeking about your religion draw you even further off course from being a faithful follower? Will you be able to walk away? Would you ever want to do that? How would your spouse or your family react?

On the other hand, what if your church turns on you? It is unlikely, but certainly possible. Would you be able to live with that? Again, how would that impact the people in your life?

The reason I'm extra careful with religion is that it tends to be such a powerful force in our lives. Whether it is the fear of eternal damnation or just the strong sense of community we receive from religion, the connection can be one of the strongest of your life.

Thus, while I realize it is very difficult to simply "swap religions," I do want you to study other denominations or sects that might align better with your authentic self before you start taking actions that may result in the consequences discussed above. Lord knows (no pun intended), there is no shortage of churches out there. But if you are heavily involved in a church that you're questioning, you might benefit from having a new community at the ready should your challenges lead to an impasse.

Again, I cannot emphasize enough that this process should be undertaken with the guidance of a spiritual leader (or leaders). Ask the questions. In fact, ask the same questions of multiple clergy. Take notes. Analyze the answers. Be honest with yourself about yourself. And then, my friend, make the best decision for you and your soul. I understand what a huge undertaking this is. That's why you got a whole separate chapter on it.

But let's get this started, shall we? Here are some steps to guide you.

What principle(s) of your religion trouble you the most?

What is it about those particular rules that bother you so much?

Who have you talked to about it?

Have you spoken to a clergyperson?

Aside from the clergy at your own church, are there other local clergy you want to speak with?

Do you think you should consult clergy from multiple religions? If so, what other religion(s) do you want to explore on this issue?

Have you studied the scriptures from your religion on this issue?

Have you studied other religious texts on this issue?

What is the most respectful way you can approach the topic with clergy?

How will you respond if you get an answer you don't like?

How would your life change if you decided you needed to leave your home church?

How would your life change if you decided you needed to leave your religion?

Do you have friends you can talk to about this issue who aren't necessarily religious? How might their perspective on the issue differ from your own?

Good luck, my friends. This is an important journey, no matter where you land.

"Genuine relationships depend first on a healthy relationship with ourselves."

—Sonja Choquette

Five

Relationships

When I set out to write this book, I had a solid outline. In addition to that, I had a really good idea of what I was going to say in each chapter. I didn't write the book in chronological order. I wrote some of the later chapters first and then I came back and wrote some of the chapters that appear early on.

For the most part, the writing came easily. I had been thinking about, studying, coaching, and taking notes on each concept for years. With a few minor hiccups, the words just flowed. And then I sat down to write this chapter, which was originally titled "Unhealthy Relationships." I will admit, the words stopped flowing.

Actually, the *correct* words stopped flowing and I began my walk down memory lane of all of the unhealthy relationships that I had in my life. Perhaps not surprisingly, I was able to pinpoint why each one of them did not work. I was able to discern exactly why the *other person* sucked and why the relationship was never meant to be because of *their* inadequacies. Yay me! Or . . . maybe not. Please understand, the sarcasm is a reflection of the knowledge that I am the common denominator in all of my failed relationships. It has not escaped me, nor did I expect it to escape you, Sherlock.

Have you ever tried to define what an ideal relationship is? It is hard! People are messy and unpredictable. Then you throw in some miscommunication and it is just a pile of goo that never seems to work.

Do you disagree? You should try it. In fact, I dare you to sit down and write a paragraph about healthy vs. unhealthy relationships. You did it? Ok, good. Now read it back to yourself and ask if it applies to everyone you know. My guess is that it doesn't. And why it doesn't is because we all have different needs and definitions of what a relationship is.

Is an unhealthy relationship characterized by fighting? Some couples hash things out quite well through raised voices and excessive gesturing.

Is your healthy relationship defined by monogamy? Good for you. The truth is, monogamy doesn't work for everyone. Some people, in fact, thrive within polyamory.

Maybe you think a healthy relationship is one where each person lifts the other up. That's not a bad concept but what about those times when we're so down ourselves (due to grief, illness, or some other external factor) that we can't possibly lift another? Does that mean our relationships have to end in those times?

I told you, it's not that easy. The concept of a "healthy relationship" is highly subjective. So, I decided to drop the description—"healthy vs. unhealthy"—and chose instead to just focus on relationships. And, as the opening quote suggests, relationships begin and end with YOU. Let's talk about it.

Defining relationships

Before we start tearing into our relationship with relationships, let's first define the term. Like any good researcher, I chose to start with the dictionary definition. I found three alternative meanings:

"The way in which two or more concepts, objects, or people are connected, or the state of being connected."

"The state of being connected by blood or marriage."

"The way in which two or more people or groups regard and behave toward each other."

There are a couple of things I love about those definitions. First, the idea that a relationship is a state of being *connected*. Think about that for a moment. Whether we're talking about a romantic relationship, a friendship, a professional relationship, or the relationship with a family member, all of those things require connection with another person. That's a beautiful thing.

I also like the concept that a relationship is defined by the way two people behave toward one another. If you and I behave intimately, that's one kind of relationship. If my behavior suggests that I want to tear you down and belittle you, that's another. Think about the very best relationship of your entire life. How did you and that person *behave* toward one another? And how did that work out for you?

Interesting concepts, to be sure. I want to be clear as we head through this chapter, however, that when I discuss relationships, I'm not only talking about romantic relationships. I'm talking about you and any other person you are connected with. If you want to focus on one or more relationships in your life as we walk down this path, great. Just know that you're not limited to thinking about your boyfriend, spouse, mother, etc.

Another tip: I honestly don't want you spending too much time thinking about those other people at all. Sure, they're important and the work you do within this chapter will undoubtedly impact those connections. But first and foremost, I want you to think about your relationship with YOU. That's because as I hashed out the concepts I wanted to set forth in this chapter, I realized that none of us can achieve a "healthy relationship" with another unless and until we have a healthy relationship with ourselves.

What does that look like?

Connecting with yourSELF

How connected are you to you? I mean, sure, you're stuck in your body and you're stuck with your mind. But have you taken the time to really connect with yourself; to have a relationship with yourself?

For starters, I'm going to ask you to dig *really* deep. Specifically, I want you to focus on the definitions of love and connection that you learned as a child. Your parents/caregivers were the absolute first and most important model that you had for loving and connecting with others in this world. So, what did they teach you? Trigger warning: this could get messy.

To illustrate the point, I'm going to recall stories from my own childhood, as well as the stories of a few trusted friends who were brave enough to go through this exercise with me. But this is my book and we'll start with me. First, however, I want to talk about a concept you read about in Chapter 2—*expectations*.

The root of relationship expectations

Like most people, I received different messages about love from my mother and my father. Nonetheless, the common themes between them were independence and detachment. It wasn't that they didn't love me, it's that life was hard and people were busy so there was no need to send constant reminders of that fact. I can see that same message through multiple generations in my family. The fact that I had a house and food on the table was to be my reassurance.

Both my dad and mom were very good at communicating (either through words or actions) that I should never put my guard down because people would only disappoint me. The manner in which they loved me continually reinforced this messaging. There wasn't a lot of coddling in my household, but there were plenty of reminders of the importance of independence. Trust no one, be strong, fend for yourself, don't cry, you can only rely on yourself. It sounds like a harsh message, but please don't get me wrong, I am grateful for that lesson. It has made me who I am today. Oh sure, I have had to deal with the fallout of that messaging as well, but I am always thankful for its gifts.

That may not be the warm and fuzzy childhood memory we all wish we had. But it gave me a lesson about love, didn't it? In many respects, it taught me what I *didn't* want. I didn't always want to be independent. It felt bad. It felt scary. It felt lonely, especially when there was no one to turn to when I couldn't muster my own strength. There was a hole that could not be filled with independence. As a result, I unconsciously sought out relationships where I was needed in one way or another. There was a co-dependency aspect in me that was very much in need of that. And, because I did not know how to love myself in the manner I needed, I would end up feeling loved only when I was giving to someone else, regardless of whether what they asked from me was fair or appropriate.

That was the love I needed as a child. Nonetheless, I remained consciously attached to the notion of being an independent woman and remained steadfast in defining myself as such. As I look back now at my litany of unhealthy relationships, I see that this internal struggle was always in the way.

Then I went through the hard work of connecting with myself. What did the child-me want and need in order to truly feel love? One of the things I came to understand was that independence was a gift I could give myself. Being self-sustaining was important to me.

Yet, I kept searching for someone who would "prove" their love by needing me, demanding more of me than was healthy, and stealing my independence. I came to expect that every relationship would proceed this way. It never occurred to me that I could be independent, free from control by a partner, and still feel loved.

Therein lies the problem. I used the expectations formed in my childhood to guide how I dealt with my partners. I strove for independence yet chose partners who gave me anything but that. In some part of my brain, I was still that junior-high girl who just wanted to have someone put an arm around her. But I had been taught that that warm embrace meant giving up my own control. It had to mean a lack of independence. It had to mean I'd let my guard down. And that, according to childhood-me, was a notion that had to be rejected. Is it any wonder so many of my relationships ended in discord?

Fast forward to today, when I am more connected with myself and the messaging I internalized as a child about love. Now, I understand that I can *both*: (1) love myself for being independent, *AND* (2) let someone else love me as an independent woman. I don't expect them to need me in unhealthy ways in order to show love.

Let's look at another example of messaging from childhood. My friend (we'll call her Maria), grew up in a two-parent home. Her dad, she explained at the outset of our discussion, had provided what she termed "unconditional love." It wasn't that he never disciplined her; he did. It's just that she knew that no matter what happened in life, her dad would love her. As she grew older, she formed expectations about what that unconditional love looked like.

For example, if she ever needed *anything* fixed or improved, her dad would be there. Painting houses, fixing up backyards, helping with the down payment on a house . . . you name it, her dad showed up to help.

She also watched her dad do that for other people. Pretty much if anyone needed anything, her dad would show up to lend a hand. That is simply how he gave love. And, consequently, it is how her childhood-self internalized what love was supposed to look like.

So, as Maria aged and had her own litany of relationships, she often found herself disappointed by her partners. She had become someone who gave and gave and gave of herself (like her dad) but was always disappointed when her partners did not return the favors. All of her relationships felt one-sided and, relatively quickly, she would tire of not receiving "unconditional love."

She bailed on one relationship after her partner chastised her for not folding shirts correctly. How could that person be mad at her when she had taken the time to lovingly tackle the couple's laundry? In another relationship, she felt like she was constantly doing errands for the other person, only to have that person tell her they wanted to stay together but date other people at the same time. How could that be when she was giving so much of herself to the other person? Wasn't that enough?

Maria, like so many of us, was completely disconnected from her childhood expectations of love. Her dad had given so much of himself . . . why couldn't she find another person who would do the same? Especially when she was so ready, able, and willing to do that for someone else?

The problem, as Maria and I discussed, is that she needed to fulfill that love expectation *for herself.*

Instead of constantly giving to her partners with varying expectations about what was to be given in return, she needed to focus her internal messaging about love on herself. If she could give herself unconditional love . . . if she could run errands for herself, pull weeds for herself, take care of herself when she was sick . . . then she would not have to place those very subjective expectations on her partners. Once she was loving herself unconditionally, and doing all sorts of favors for herself, she could open herself to allow another person to love her in a way that was comfortable and natural *for them and for her.*

One more example before we turn the focus onto you. This one comes from my friend Michelle. Michelle was raised by her mother, who was an extremely religious woman. Her mother gave her all sorts of messaging about love as a child.

For one thing, Michelle learned that she was never, ever supposed to call a boy or communicate with a boy unless he communicated first. Another rule was that she could never wear makeup because it invited "unwanted" sexual attention. In short, Michelle learned that the only way she could ever be worthy of love (from her mother or anyone else) was if she was a good girl. She was never to be aggressive in her desire for attention from others. Rather, the way to remain chaste and good was to wait for someone else to approach her in her most natural state.

You can imagine how this translated into Michelle's adult life. For one thing, she never got over the fact that she was not supposed to express desire. Thus, while other people were out engaging in normal communications (like when new friends or new love-interests call and text one another, equally), Michelle would always sit back and wait for the other person to contact her. In her mind, if they stopped making the first move (which, predictably, they all did), they simply didn't love (or even like) her. And, in the rare instances when Michelle would make first-contact, she would tell herself she was being "slutty" or "desperate"—just like her mom had taught her.

In those instances where Michelle did fall into serious relationships, they tended to be with highly controlling people—those who, like her mom, would tell her what was "good" and "bad" behavior within the relationship. She knew that the only path to love was to be good in order to please that external influence.

Perhaps not surprisingly, this became harder and harder for

Michelle to sustain as she grew into a strong, educated, professional woman. Often, her disdain for her own obedience would suddenly and forcefully come out as anger toward her partner. Within short order, that relationship would be over.

So, when Michelle set out to connect with herself as an adult, she had some pretty heavy childhood messaging to wade through. She knew that in order to give and receive love, she needed to feel "good" on some level. What Michelle had to do for herself, however, was become the final arbiter of what "good" and "bad" meant for her. She had to stop expecting someone else to fill that role for her.

Well, guess what? As she did that very hard work, Michelle eventually found a way for her to feel "good" about herself that had nothing to do with anyone else's expectations. In fact, feeling good about herself became a constant source of pleasure in her life. Not shockingly, her definition of "good" looked nothing like her mother's. And that's ok. The journey, as you'll recall, is all about taking those childhood messages about love and making them work for you as an adult.

Time for YOU to connect with child-YOU

Ok, you've read a couple of examples of other people's struggles and now it's time for you to do some hard work on you. I want you to really take the time to connect with you.

As you probably surmised, that begins by connecting with the messaging you received (and internalized) about love as a child. Get out a pen and some paper. We're going to do this right. Go through the following list of questions and write out your answers:

1. Who raised you? (If you were raised by more than one central caretaker, you probably want to go through this exercise with respect to EACH individual who shaped your young life).

2. How did the person who raised you show you love? (Maybe they provided for you, gave you hugs, taught you discipline . . . that's up to you to define. But I really

want you to think about how and when you felt loved as a child).

3. What did you learn about love from the way it was shown to you? (E.g., did you learn you needed to be independent, passive, loud, etc.? The possibilities are endless).

4. What were the conditions to you receiving love as a child? (Did you have to behave a certain way in order to receive love? Did you feel unconditionally loved? Did you feel love when you achieved certain grades at school?)

5. Now that you've thought about the messaging you received, try to sum it up in a sentence or two.

6. Got it? Good. Now, have you ever expected that another person in your life (friend, partner, family member, etc.) love you in a way that dovetails with your childhood messaging? If so, please write out how you've done that.

7. Have you ever tried to fulfill your need for that childhood form of love *for yourself*? If yes, how?

8. If your answer to the last question was "no," how do you think you could love yourself in a way that satisfies your own internal, childhood-based need for love?

Those are big questions and I expect you to take your time and answer them in the most authentic way possible. Once you've done that, please come back for some more reflection, questioning, and hard work.

Connecting with adult-YOU is important too

Obviously, I believe the messaging we all received about love as a child is critical to how we give and receive love as adults. But I also understand that our adult experiences are equally important for connecting with our true selves.

So, let's do a little work around that. For this part of the exercise, I don't want you to go any deeper than your gut feelings about who you are right now, today. Ready? Get that pen and paper back out. Let's do this.

1. What pleases you, emotionally?

2. What makes you smile?

3. What makes you cringe?

4. What stimulates your appetite for knowledge?

5. How do you like to be treated?

6. And, perhaps most importantly, what are your core values?

[Hint: It is okay if you are not completely clear on your core values yet. Do the best you can and we will dive into how you can define those for yourself in Chapter 10, *Be Bold*.]

Let's talk through some of these things. How did you respond to the question "what pleases you, emotionally"? Maybe you said that calmness pleases you emotionally. I get it. But now ask yourself, are you achieving calm within your relationships with others? Do you have it in your relationship with yourself?

Run through that same exercise for each of the questions above. You should be able to get through most of these with relative ease. That's not to say that the questions aren't important—they are. But if you don't have gut-level responses to questions 1–5, we've got a lot more work to do. And that's ok . . .

Remember, you're just trying to connect with your own adult feelings at this point—your likes and dislikes. Don't make this hard until it has to be. Your feelings are often an indicator of a much deeper core value.

Ok, now is the time to make it harder. I want to focus on your answers about core values because I suspect those may have been the greatest struggle for you. Let's dissect how being connected to your core personal values will help you have a relationship with yourself which, in turn, will help you have relationships with others. I'll use a couple of my values as examples.

As you learned above, one of my truly personal, personal values is independence. I need to be able to care for myself, I need to be able to entertain myself, and I truly dislike anyone trying to control any part of my life. Part of my connection to me is fostering my sense of independence. Yes, this is a value that was formed in my childhood but it remains a core part of me to this day.

So, what would happen if I met someone (a really *cute* someone, by the way) and that person was terribly co-dependent? What if, once we started dating, they always wanted to be by my side? What if they planned out our social calendar a month in advance without consulting me? What if they went shopping for me and bought all sorts of outfits they thought I'd look good in? Sound familiar? Well, I told you earlier that I had a habit of partnering with very co-dependent individuals.

But remember, this person is CUTE. They are also funny and engaging and intelligent—traits that are very important to me in a partner. What should I do? I'm highly connected to my core value of independence, yet I've met this amazing person who threatens my ability to exercise that independence.

First, when it comes to independence, I need to acknowledge and process the fact that this value comes from my childhood (see above). I'm bringing it up again here because, from time to time, connection with ourselves will necessarily involve our childhood messaging AND the beliefs we've formed as adults. Since we already talked earlier about how I've dealt with my childhood messaging around the notion of independence, let's now dive into how my adult self plays into it.

So, I've met this amazing person who threatens my independence. What are my options? Obviously, I could run for the hills. But they are *really* cute and funny and I'd like to give this a shot.

What would happen if I communicated my core values? What if I gave them the chance to:

See my relationship with myself;

Understand the importance of independence in my life; and

Loosen up a little bit?

There are really only two valid outcomes: Either we adjust our relationship in a way that allows me to stay connected to me or we don't work.

Actually, there is one more option. I could ignore my relationship with myself and allow this cute, funny, intelligent person to control my every move. Sure it would be fun at first, but then how long do you think that would last? Once the oxytocin wears off, I'm probably going to be mad at myself (and resent them) for having lost my connection with me. And, in this instance, it's a connection to both childhood-me and adult-me. So, I'm a double loser.

Let's look at another example that is less "all-or-nothing." One of my other core values is creativity. I'm principally concerned that I am always creating something, but it would be nice if the people around me were also creative. So, let's say I meet the same person we talked about above. They are still cute, funny, charming, and intelligent. But in this scenario, they are an accountant—all about numbers and things being black and white. They don't have a creative bone in their body.

Again, I have to look at my relationship with me.

Here, I have no hard-core childhood messaging around creativity to deal with. Does my drive toward creativity have to spill over into my partner or can I have creative outlets in other, non-romantic relationships? I'm thinking the latter. But I would only know that by being so deeply connected with who I am and how I define that for myself.

The key here, of course, is using that connection—that *relationship*—with yourself in making decisions about your relationships with others. I mentioned oxytocin earlier. That's a real thing and it's powerful. It can make us do crazy things or make poor decisions in the moment. The best thing you can do for yourself is be armed with knowledge about you—before you are under the influence. Because once that oxytocin kicks in, it is near impossible to walk a straight line.

Behave yourSELF

Remember that other key definition of relationships: "*The way in which two or more people or groups regard and behave toward each other*"? Once you start focusing on your relationship with yourself, you have to ask: how do you behave toward you? Because, I'm here to tell you that how *you* treat *you* has everything to do with how others treat you.

Do you take care of yourself? Do you drink too much? Smoke? Eat right? Do you exercise? Do you meditate? Do you allow yourself to take long baths just to unwind? In essence, do you do things that are good for you?

To understand this concept, let's put the shoe on the other foot and take a look at how other people in your life treat themselves. Let's say you have a friend, we'll call her Robyn. Robyn is a consummate party girl. She's up until 2 in the morning most days. She parties a *lot*. She eats pizza for breakfast (at noon) and has an endless stream of romantic partners. Nonetheless, you like her. She's funny and you can always count on her to show you a good time.

But when do you call Robyn? Do you call her when you are sad and need to bare your soul? Do you call her when you feel like spending a quiet afternoon at the art museum? Or do you call her when you feel like partying, knowing that she'll always be down for a good time? Chances are, it's the last option. Robyn's relationship with herself has taught you that you can treat her similarly. So, when you feel like letting loose, that's who you call.

Your relationship with you—the way *you* behave toward yourself— also informs how other people will behave toward you. Let's say you are financially irresponsible. You never met a bill you liked to pay on time. Yet, you're also furious because your mom treats you like a child, even though you're 42 years old. Well, what do you expect? You behave in a way toward yourself that tells other people you're not responsible. Your mom is simply reacting to that. Your relationship with you tells her everything she needs to know about her relationship with you. You need to be babied and she does that for you. Why are you mad at her?

Now, envision someone who has their shit together. They're steadily employed, they pay their bills on time, they dress well, they eat well, they exercise regularly, meditate, and they have a ton of money in the bank. In other words, they behave very nicely toward themselves. How do you treat that person? Is that a person you're going to hurl insults at? Probably not. Their care for themselves has taught you how to treat them.

So, now comes the hard part. I want you to think of the people in your life who have treated you poorly. Have someone in mind? Ok, now ask yourself if they learned to treat you that way by observing the way you treat you. I know, it's hard. I never promised this book would be easy.

To lighten things up a bit, now I want you to think about someone who treats you really well. What did you teach them that led them to believe they should treat you that way? What behaviors toward yourself did you exhibit that let them think you deserve to be treated as special?

Let's go back to my friend Maria for a minute. We talked about her earlier in this chapter when we were discussing how we all need to connect with the messaging we received about love as children. You'll recall that Maria was blessed with a father who gave what she described as "unconditional love." That's amazing. Yet, as great as that was, Maria struggles as an adult because she expects her partners and friends to also offer that kind of love. That's highly unrealistic.

To illustrate this point, let's assume for a minute that Maria continues down the path of expecting others to provide her with unconditional love.

When she doesn't get it (and really, who can provide that?) she'll stomp her feet and pound her fists and generally act like a child. If you've been paying attention, that's exactly what she is in that moment. Although Maria may think she is providing unconditional love to the people in her life, she is actually providing love with pretty heavy strings attached. She expects the people in her life to treat her the same way and, if they don't, she lashes out.

When she behaves that way, however, remember that she is actually teaching the other person how to treat her. After she acts out for not receiving the kind of love, she thinks she deserves, the people in her life are less likely to treat her like an adult who wants to be loved and more likely to treat her like a child who needs to be avoided.

Rather than causing this downward spiral, Maria can actually save herself. What if Maria behaved toward herself as if unconditional love was the only option? What if she forgave herself every time she perceived that she'd done something wrong? What if she took time out of her day to help herself around the house? What if she ran her own errands and painted her own living room and did all those things for herself that she always associated with unconditional love for others?

Not only is Maria likely to have a happier life with herself, but the way she is behaving toward herself is teaching others how to treat her. Perhaps ironically, by giving herself unconditional love, Maria is showing other people that she is worthy of it. It's kind of simple and kind of mind-blowing all at the same time, right?

So, now it's time for you to start thinking about how you treat you. As you may have suspected, I have an exercise for you.

To start off, I want you to make two lists. The first is a list of five behaviors you exhibit toward yourself that would make people believe you should be treated well. The second, of course, is a list of five behaviors you exhibit toward yourself that would lead people to believe they can treat you poorly. By all means, don't stop at five if you're on a roll. Really think about how you treat yourself.

Before I let you off the hook, however, I want to add a third list to the mix. I want you to list five behaviors you could enact today that would show you unconditional love toward yourself. Because in all honesty, I think Maria's dad was onto something. I believe that the more we act with unconditional love toward ourselves, the more love will come rolling back our way—and the more love we can authentically give to others.

Now is the time that I want you to put the book down. Take the next few days to really study those lists. Are there additional things you could do to teach other people to treat you well? Conversely, are there ways that you behave toward yourself that you should cut out if you want to be treated better? Are there more things you could do for you to show unconditional love? Once you have absorbed those lists, start to put them into practice.

I know, it is terrifying. But you deserve it, don't you?

"You don't have to pretend to know me and I don't have to pretend to like you."

—Christina M. Ellis

Six

Social Media

Yeah, that's right. I quoted myself to open this chapter. I did so because it's one of the best lines that I ever delivered to another person *and* I did so in the context of social media. I said it to someone I met casually.

After we had chatted for a while, she asked to connect with me on Facebook. I didn't know her that well and I didn't feel like opening up my life to her, so I declined. She was highly offended. That was everything I needed to know about that person.

"You don't have to pretend to know me and I don't have to pretend to like you," I blurted out, almost instinctively. Later, I realized that my somewhat abrupt comment really exemplifies how I feel about social media in general. The ideas of friendship or true connection in that setting are so false as to border on the ludicrous.

To prove my point, I once spent around two months trying to rack up as many "friends" as I could on social media sites. If anyone (and I mean *anyone*) sent me a friend request, I accepted it without question. I sent my own friend requests to anyone and everyone. Sadly, only two people responded to my request by asking, "how do I know you?" They were both older (and wiser) individuals.

Nonetheless, I used my standard line on them (for purposes of this experiment, at least). "Oh," I'd say, "we're both friends with so-and-so. I figure meeting you on social media is just like meeting you at a cocktail party at so-and-so's house." It worked. Neither rejected my request.

By the time my "experiment" was over, I had between 3,000 to 4,000 "friends." And guess what? I didn't know a damn thing about them, and they didn't know a damn thing about me. That's not friendship, that's hoarding. And it literally made me sick. Therefore, when I set out to write this book, I knew I had to add a chapter on social media; its dangers, its limited benefits, and how it might fit into an intentional life.

After all, according to the Pew Research Center, roughly 70% of Americans are using social media. It's time somebody talked about using it intentionally.

Sure, social media has some benefits

Whenever I start a conversation about the ills of social media, most people give me the same response: "Well, I'd never be in touch with my [cousins, aunts, high-school friends, college roommates, etc.] if I didn't connect with them on social media." Ok, I get it. And I still call bullshit.

Twenty years ago, we all kept in touch with the people we *wanted* to keep in touch with. Period. We wrote letters, we went to lunches, we picked up the phone. During those connections, we talked about significant life events like marriages, divorces, childbirth, losses, jobs, holidays, and the like. We had real *conversations* about the things that mattered to us.

Today, I know within seconds if my third-grade classmate's cat coughed up a hairball. Or that my high school vice principal is having a hard time getting to sleep. Or that some person I don't even know but somehow became my "friend" is watching *Game of Thrones* in their pajamas and loving it. WTF? To add insult to injury, it seems that everyone is talking AT us rather than engaging *with* us.

Oh wait, this was the part of the chapter where I was going to be positive about social media.

I guess this is as positive as I can be.

I just don't believe that real connections are forged via 22-word snippets of someone's life. If you really wanted to know about that person or they really wanted to know about you, you'd call each other. But go ahead and keep telling yourself that it's a good thing to be "connected" with everyone you've ever encountered. Go ahead and passively view your aunt's new relationship rather than calling and talking to her. At least you know what's up in her life without having to make an effort at real connection.

I know, I know . . . I'm pretty harsh when it comes to social media. And I really do see some of the good things about it. For instance, it is a great (and often free) way for businesses to connect with new clients. It is a good place for professionals to post blogs, articles, and other content that positions them as a thought leader in their field. It is a way that fans of a certain product (or political candidate) can share their knowledge of whatever (or whomever) it is they love. I do get all that. And if you are successfully using social media to boost your business, good for you!

Now, back to my more curmudgeonly side . . .

The fallacy of social media

One of my biggest problems with social media is the pressure it creates to curate the perfect life. We feel compelled to prove to the world that we're happy, healthy, dieting, sober, exercising, or whatever other thing makes us feel ok. But don't we all know by now that 90% of that is just a fairytale?

I was reminded of this recently when I had a visit (like a real, in-person visit) from an old friend, her husband, and their two-year-old son. I had been looking forward to their visit because I found myself fascinated with the life they had been presenting on social media.

For one thing, they were a bit of an "older" couple to have such a young child. Shortly after the baby was born, they decided to sell everything, purchase an RV, and simply travel the United States.

From their social media posts, it looked like all they did was travel from national park to national park. At each stop, they would take amazing hikes and expose their young son to all the outdoorsy beauty this country has to offer.

Every picture showed them smiling, laughing, and looking tan and fit. There was a part of me that thought perhaps they'd found the perfect life.

Then they arrived at my house. The adults seemed to pour out of the camper like cold molasses. They both looked dusty, road-weary, and blurry-eyed. The little one, relieved to be freed from the cage of the road, scrambled out of the RV and was instantly into everything in my house. I could tell the parents would love nothing more than to have me keep him alive without their input or oversight—even if it was just for a few minutes.

As I talked to my friend, I learned that having a child had been a nightmare for the couple. The kid hadn't slept more than 45 minutes at a stretch for his whole life—not one single time! Mom and dad were exhausted, their sex life was non-existent, and they hardly talked anymore. The trip around the country in a camper was more about both parents losing their jobs than it was about forging an exciting life for their son. In short, their entire world was a pit of depression and stress.

It just so happened, however, that they showed up at my house on their son's second birthday. I was prepared with streamers, balloons, candles, and a cake. My friend and I prepared a perfect birthday scene for the little one. As soon as everything was in place, guess what happened?

That's right, mom and dad locked arms around their son, lit the candles, put on loving, happy smiles, and had me take pictures of the scene from their phones. Within minutes, those deliriously happy photos had made their way to social media.

Back in the real world, the couple returned to being miserable as soon as the posts were complete. They were bickering, the smiles were gone, the kid was crying, and everyone just seemed to want to get away from each other. What a contrast from the family that appeared online!

Sadly, I don't think my friends' experience is unusual. Social media is like a high school yearbook that we get to publish for ourselves. And most of us act about high-school age when we do it. We put on fake smiles, nice clothes, and present our greatest moments to the world. Rarely do we present our real selves—the ones who don't get out of their pajamas all day, eat nachos for breakfast, or yell at our kids.

So, why do we do this? Principally, we do it because we want to be liked. We want others to believe we've made it. We don't want anyone to know we're actually struggling. And the more we present these fallacies to the world, the more distant we become from the people we actually love. We don't let them see us and love us for who we are and that, in my estimation, is a crying shame.

Vague-booking, AKA, using social media for attention

Remember back in high school when, from time to time, somebody would show up to school with a sad face and furrowed brow? They'd slowly shuffle from class to class with their heads down and their books held tightly against their chest. Remember how everybody would ask with concern, "what's wrong," only to have that person flatly reply, "Nothing"?

Notwithstanding their vagueness about the situation, they would garner all sorts of attention throughout the day as people tried to pry the details of their despondency. In hindsight and (hopefully) with a greater degree of emotional intelligence than we had in high school, we can see that those people often just loved the attention they got from acting upset. Well, guess what? That same thing happens with grown-ass adults on social media all the time.

This was exemplified for me during my experiment of collecting as many "friends" as I could. One day, I logged onto Facebook and was immediately drawn to a post by a "friend" I had never met. He posted a picture of himself sitting in his car with a gun on his lap. The text of his post gave a vague reference to his desire to end his life.

What am I supposed to do with this? Hundreds of people responded to him. Many with replies along the lines of "I know I don't know you personally, but believe me when I say things really will get better!" or "We love you, don't do it!" or "You are amazing in so many ways". I thought to myself, "huh?" Others gave the number for the National Suicide Hotline. All were concerned. At first, I was concerned. But, was I *really*?

According to the American Foundation for Suicide Prevention, over 47,000 people take their own lives in the United States each year. Blessedly, I've never known one of them and there was nothing I could have ever done to prevent any of those deaths. Was this guy somehow different because he was a "friend" on social media? Would any of my wise words in response to his post have changed the outcome?

This is a harsh analogy, I know, but it begs the question—how friendly do we need to be with our false social media "friends"? And how far can we stretch our compassion?

What if all 4,000 of my "friends" had made similar posts that day? Was I supposed to try to save all of them, even though I didn't know them?

Two days later, this same gentleman made an innocuous, good-natured post. To my knowledge, he never said another word about suicide. Yet, his frightful, public offering made hundreds of people stop what they were doing and feign concern.

I'm sure he got some sort of personal satisfaction from that. I was angry, not because he threatened something so serious and did not actually do it, but because he caused so much unnecessary drama and fear amongst his peers . . . excuse me, "friends." That is the day I deleted my four thousand fake friends.

Social media's wholesale dilution of relationships

If you think my reaction to the story in the last section is overly harsh, I would invite you to consider science and history. Biology has programmed us to take whatever steps are necessary to propagate our own genes (i.e., ensure the survival of our offspring). History tells us that, until very recently, we have formed bonds and relationships that enhance our chances of doing so.

I don't need to go any further back than the time when our country was formed to make this point. Back then, Native Americans were, in large part, living in discrete communities centered around family and community. Similarly, once Europeans arrived on this continent, they tended to reside in townships where families would live and grow for generations.

Aside from major socioeconomic shifts like the gold rush or the Great Depression, people mostly lived in the same place their entire lives. Multiple generations would reside on the same property. Older family members were cared for by the younger ones. Young couples were expected to have children who, in turn, were expected to contribute to the family business—whether that was farming or shop keeping or anything else.

Friendships were formed around church, family, and community. Everyone knew everyone else. If someone in the community needed help, others tended to pitch in and help. Gossip existed, to be sure (look no further than the Salem witch trials to prove this) but, by and large, people had true and meaningful relationships with those around them.

The first major wave of invention to change this dynamic was transportation. From the transcontinental railroad (built in the 1800s) to the interstate highway system (constructed in the 1900s), these advances in technology allowed people to travel and move to distant locations with relative ease. As a consequence, communication and relationships changed.

Nonetheless, people still communicated with actual loved ones through letters and, eventually, by telephone. There were no networks of strangers to inform the populace of everyone's everyday activities.

Not until the internet came into existence did that major relationship dynamic change. In 1991, the World Wide Web became available to the public. In short order, people formed chat rooms where they could converse with others who had similar interests but weren't necessarily friends. I know a couple of people who found a degree of trouble by communicating in these new-fangled, often-anonymous venues.

By the early 2000s, social media sites like MySpace and Facebook cropped up and they changed the notion of "friendship" forever. Suddenly, our lives were on display for a whole new audience. Whereas, in the past, tacit friendships formed in grammar school or high school naturally dwindled with time, suddenly we were inviting those people back into our homes to participate in our every move. Worse yet, we were inviting complete strangers into our lives and our children's lives, sharing the most intimate details of our physical, mental, and emotional health.

Meanwhile, letter writing has become a lost art. Long, intimate phone calls are few and far between. Instead of having those meaningful connections, you become aware of things like the fact that your secretary from 20 years ago lost her cat. A secretary, mind you, that you haven't talked to in at least 19 years. And then you spend precious moments deciding whether you should "connect" with her over the loss by giving her a "sad face emoji" or a "heart emoji."

While all of this happens, real life slips away. Real relationships get lost. Time escapes us.

Don't believe me? Let's start by looking at a few key statistics:

According to the United States Census Bureau, there are over 327 million people in the United States.

As noted above, the Pew Research Center tells us that over 70% of Americans use some sort of social media (that's 228,900,000 of us, for those keeping track).

Broadbandsearch.net reports that the average person spends 144 minutes on social media each and every day.

If you do the math based on these three simple stats, you come up with some shocking insight about our collective use of social media as Americans. For example:

We spend 32,961,600,000 minutes on social media each day.

That equates to **62,712 years** worth of time spent on social media each and every day. Just in America.

Imagine the advances we could make in science, health, industry, art, and *relationships* if we poured that time into something more meaningful than deciding whether to tell our secretary from decades ago that we're sorry her cat died.

Imagine the impact I could have if I volunteered 144 minutes every single day to my local suicide prevention hotline rather than looking at pictures of some unknown "friend" with a gun on his lap. Imagine the impact all of us could make if we spent 144 minutes a day doing something even slightly more meaningful than scrolling through social media posts made by random strangers and the people we knew in junior high.

Just to bring this full circle, I want to share an experience that happened to me not long ago. I was sitting at dinner with someone who was very special in my life.—a person with whom I was supposed to share the deepest level of love. I was regurgitating the play by play of a pretty rough day and taking the opportunity to let a little stress wash away, when their phone made the tell-tale "ding" that means a new Facebook message had arrived. Guess what happened next? They turned their attention away from me, picked up the phone, and looked at the message. Now, I am hoping that this slight has never happened to you, but sadly, my guess is that it has.

Isn't that the perfect example of how diluted our relationships have become *because of* social media? Our attention is so scattered across so many people that we can't make it through a real-life conversation with someone special in our life without being distracted. Now, I don't know what kind of message they received, but I know it wasn't important enough that we had to jump up from the table and run to the hospital (the only kind of message, in my opinion, that would warrant the disruption to our dinner).

If you don't want to cut down on your social media use wholeheartedly, how about this? How about you don't let it distract you when you're in the presence of another real person? How about you make it a rule in your house that no one can look at their phones, tablets, or computers during family meals? What if you left your phone in your car when you went out to lunch with someone? If we could all do these few simple things, it would at least be a small step toward the preservation of real relationships.

Social media is like cotton candy—it tastes good, but there is no substance there. If you like cotton candy and you want to eat it, fine. Just don't expect it to nourish you.

The impact of social media on other aspects of our lives

Do you know anyone who has worked in the service industry for many years? If so, ask them how social media has changed their business.

I did this recently with a friend of mine who has worked in the same pub since around 2005. Here's what she had to say:

"Well, people used to come to our place to talk, laugh, and have a good time. The place was always loud, and people had a lot of fun. Today, most people are just sitting across from other people staring at their phones. Or they're sitting at the bar by themselves, staring at their phones. Nine times out of ten, when I walk past, I notice they're scrolling through Facebook or Instagram. There are days when the place is filled, but it is deadly quiet, except for the music. It's because everyone is on their damn phone."

She went on to explain that not only is this a sad comment on our society, but that it has impacted her financially. You see, when people used to visit a restaurant without the distraction of social media, they would eat, pay their check, and leave.

These days, they often linger long after their meal is done, just staring at their phones. As a result, she isn't turning tables as fast. It doesn't take a genius to figure out that all that lingering results in fewer tips at the end of the day.

After our talk, I started to notice this reality all the time. It's not hard to observe. Just walk into a coffee shop or restaurant and watch what people are doing. Most are glued to screens. This truth really hit me not long ago when I went to a hidden little gem of a bar to watch some live music. The musician was a handsome young man playing the acoustic guitar. I enjoyed his show very much.

When he was done playing, and much to my surprise, he walked directly over to my table. I quickly started to compliment him on his set. He interrupted me. "Oh, I know you liked it," he said. "I could tell. I just wanted to tell you that I appreciate you and thank you for being the only person who actually listened to me and watched me instead of looking at your phone the whole time."

Wow. How sad for someone with that much talent to have experienced a completely disconnected audience.

Not long after that, I was out at a restaurant with a friend. I excused myself to use the restroom, which forced me to walk past the bar. When I came out of the restroom, there were six people sitting at the bar having a drink. All SIX of them were staring at their phones! I couldn't help myself—I snapped a picture of them, and said, "Ha! You are literally sitting in a place where it is encouraged to be social with other people!"

I should figure out how to collect money for all the stink-eye I received.

On a larger scale, if you've attended a stadium concert any time over the past several years, you must have noticed that everyone around you has their phone out. They're taking videos and pictures and posting them to social media right from the venue.

The problem with each of these examples is that every time we are out on the town and staring at our phones or posting to social media, *we're missing out on real life.* How many great people have you missed out on meeting because you refused to look up from your phone? How many business connections have you missed? How many amazing musical performances have you all but ignored because you were more concerned with sharing it with strangers than with actually being present for the performance?

And just to circle back to my earlier point, each time you do this, you're not just cheating yourself out of life. You're holding up the restaurant staff, offending the musician, or just downright being annoying to the people around you. But who cares? Everyone else is on their phone too!

Part of analyzing our use of social media has to include analyzing our own self-awareness. When you start doing something to the point that it impacts (and hurts) others and yourself, it's time to check in.

You should also be asking yourself what else you're missing. Ever been to a little kid's soccer game? I swear, 85% of the parents in the audience are looking at their phones. A soccer game is one thing, but what if you missed your child's first steps? Or your brother's last breath?

Significant life events are happening all around us, and we can't stop looking at posts about our old secretary's dead cat. It's that ludicrous, and it's time to change.

Are we boiling the frog?

Do you remember that old fable about boiling a frog? The ultimate premise is that if you drop a live frog into boiling water, he'll react to the heat by jumping out and away—and you'll miss out on your frog-leg dinner. If, on the other hand, you put a frog in tepid water, and slowly heat it on the stove, he'll be cooked before he ever realizes he needs to jump out.

My question to you is: are we the frog and social media the pot of water?

For the most part, social media has only been around for less than two decades. Yet, as noted, 70% of us are already using it heavily and, as a group, we're wasting over 62,000 years' worth of time every day participating in it. What is right in front of us that we're missing?

When we're looking at social media while our partner is trying to tell us something important, that's a lost connection. When we're staring at our phone instead of talking to a potential business contact on the barstool next to us, that's a lost connection. When we fail to watch our kid's play, miss the last phone call from our grandmother, or don't answer the door when the neighbor comes to introduce herself—those are all lost connections. How can we ever get those back? And is there a critical point at which we've lost all true connections and are living entirely within the false world of social media?

Social media has made it almost like everyone in America is creating their own reality TV show all the time—yet there's no producer there to edit out the bad parts or stop you from doing something too stupid.

And all the while, we're also trying to stay on top of everyone else's reality TV show. It's an information overload that has outpaced the evolutionary process. There's simply no way we can take it all in and make sense of it. So, we keep going back to it, and going back to it, and going back to it—to the tune of 2 hours and 24 minutes a day that we're spending there, on average.

What art isn't being created in that 2 hours and 24 minutes? What inventions are being put on the backburner so we can read about strangers' cats? Which soulmates never found each other because they were scrolling social media during the 2 hours and 24 minutes they were supposed to meet? Every minute of every day, you get to decide how you want to spend your time . . . your life. Are you making decisions that you will be proud of on your deathbed?

Stop looking for permission on social media to lead the life you love. Real life is happening while we're sitting in a pot of water that is getting hot. Maybe, just maybe, we should all consider jumping out before it's too late.

"It never ceases to amaze me: we all love ourselves more than other people but care more about their opinion than our own."

—*Marcus Aurelius*

Seven

Hiring So-Called Pros

Psychologists, Psychiatrists, Counselors, Licensed Clinical Social Workers, Primary Care Physicians, Shamen, Psychics, Mediums, Astrologers, etc.

If you've made it this far in your life without consulting one or more of these folks about the status of your mental health, congratulations (or my condolences, I'm not sure which).

The truth is, life is a struggle and most of us, from time to time, seek help from one of these so-called professionals. Now, don't get me wrong . . . I'm not saying that these folks are worthless or that you shouldn't go to them or anything of the sort. They can all be incredibly healthy resources and the purpose of this chapter is not to bash them.

Actually, the purpose of this chapter is to challenge you with respect to your reliance on them.

Oh! Controversial!

Not necessarily. Hear me out.

While I generally support seeking help from mental health professionals (I love my therapist), I want to make sure we're all going to them for the right reasons. I also want to help you process some of the issues you may struggle with before you ever make the call for your first appointment. At the very least, it may save you a few bucks if you have clearly defined issues before you ever lay your head on the couch.

You don't need permission

Yep, I said it. I repeated the name of this book. In my view, too many people seek out the help of so-called professionals because they want someone else to make the decisions in their life. If they go to a counselor and the counselor says, "you should leave your husband," then they are absolved from responsibility for leaving their husband. How handy!

The truth is, 9 out of 10 women who seek counseling to determine whether to leave their husbands have already made up their minds that they are going to do so. Seeing a counselor really does nothing more than give them the permission they so desperately seek in order to pack their bags.

Again—and I know I'm walking a fine line here—I'm *not* telling you *not* to seek the help of a professional when faced with something as life-changing as leaving your husband. What I am encouraging is that you give yourself permission to make that choice before you ever walk into the office.

Why?

Because the course of your life is entirely up to you. You know, in your heart of hearts, when you need to leave (or go back to school, or start antidepressant medication, or make any other major life shift). And without a doubt, most mental health professionals can supply you with tools to help you cope through the transition. But the decision? That is up to you and you alone.

Look, you could spend 14,000 hours on the therapist's couch (and I know people who have) and your therapist will never know you as well as you know you. That's because the words that come out of your mouth can be very different from what goes on inside your own mind, body, and soul.

When you're talking to a therapist, for example, you may want that person to "like" you. You may skew certain memories from your life to make yourself sound more sympathetic. Conversely, you may mask some of your greatest tragedies because you don't want to be viewed as a victim. Or perhaps, the victim status is precisely the attention you are seeking.

Whatever the case, the point is that if you just listen to yourself, you know what the answers are. This is particularly true when you're faced with a major life decision. Don't believe me? Try this exercise. First, of course, I need you to bring whatever decision is weighing you down to the front of your mind. Keep it there as you answer the following questions. Oh, and one more caveat: your answers have to be entirely about *you*.

For example, when I ask "what does your ideal life look like?" your answer cannot be "my husband would no longer gamble online every night." It might be something like "I would love to have a life free from financial worry shared with a partner who has similar goals and expectations for the future." The truth is, we cannot change anyone else's life or behavior. This has to be *your* journey.

It also has to be intensely personal. Therefore, for purposes of this exercise, I *do not* want you to write your answers down anywhere. I don't want the slightest risk that someone else might read your wildest dreams (even if they're perfectly G-rated!). Even though I often advocate writing down your answers to the questions in this book, I don't want you to do it this time. Why? Because I want you to give yourself the most pure, unfiltered, *unabashedly-you* answers possible.

Let's get started:

1. What does your ideal life look like?

2. What makes you happy about that life?

3. What burdens that you face in your current life would be absent in your ideal life?

4. What experiences from your past give you clues as to what your ideal life would look like?

5. Which people from your current life would you bring with you to your ideal life?

6. Which people would you leave behind?

7. Where would you live in your ideal life?

8. If you had to carry forward ONE of your current burdens into your new, ideal life, which one would you choose and why?

9. If you had to leave behind ONE of your great joys from your current life, which one would you choose and why?

Now, I want you to put down this book and just think about this stuff for as long as you can. Again, think of it in the context of a major decision you need to make in your life. What do your answers tell you about that decision?

Guess what? You don't need permission from anyone to make that decision. You already know what you need to do, don't you? Armed with this information, which was derived from entirely within yourself, you can now go to your counselor.

As I said earlier, that person's job is to help you in taking the steps or finding the coping mechanisms you need to get where you want to go. You have all of the answers you need inside of you right now. A professional should be helping you pull those insights from within you.

How to find the right professional for you (and breaking up with the wrong ones)

There are a few grave dangers that exist with respect to choosing a mental health professional. Let's talk about a few of them.

Given the stigma surrounding mental illness (including common maladies like depression and anxiety), people rarely ask friends and family for trusted recommendations. Consequently, we often walk into a professional's office with no solid advice as to their effectiveness.

Many sub-specialties exist and the public has no clear understanding of the differences among practitioners (for example, there are somatic therapists, cognitive behavioral therapists, hypnotherapists, etc.). Not every modality will work for every person and if you don't understand the differences, you may be disappointed.

Insurance companies often dictate who we can see without regard to who has the best training and experience to deal with our issues.

Furthermore, just because someone made it through some schooling/training and got a certificate to hang on their wall does not mean that they are particularly good at what they do. Heck, every graduating class has to have a bottom 5%, right? So, in light of all this, how in the world do you pick the right therapist or counselor for you?

My suggestion is that you treat this person just like you would treat an employee. Interview them. Ask for references and talk to those references (this may be difficult due to doctor-patient confidentiality and HIPAA but perhaps you can ask for references from other professionals). Then give them a trial run. If they don't work out—fire them.

Look, you will know pretty quickly whether or not you're going to jive with a particular individual. You either feel comfortable opening up to them or not. You feel like you can tell them the truth or not. The advice they give to you either resonates or not. And if any of those pieces don't work for you, you have the absolute right to terminate the relationship. You don't need to feel bad. You don't even need to give an explanation. You just need to stop going to that person and move on to the next.

Understanding perspective

Regardless of the type of practitioner you use, that person is necessarily going to have a different perspective on life than you. In all likelihood, they grew up in a different town or part of the country. They may be of a different gender, race, sexuality, or religion from you. They will undoubtedly have had vastly different life experiences from you.

And just like you, all of those things have shaped their lives and their perspective on things. Unless you're going to your identical twin for therapy (never a good idea, BTW), they will necessarily look at the world through a different lens.

That said, many practitioners are trained to try to understand your perspective and to counsel you from that place. If they don't—if they are simply doling out advice based on their own unique perspective—be very wary.

I feel like I need to add clarification again. I'm not saying your practitioner should never give out advice. That's a part of their job, right? What I'm saying is if that advice comes with a statement like "Well, I was in your situation once and I'll tell you what I did . . . " then they probably aren't worth their salt.

Additionally, if your practitioner is different from you in a core way—say ethnicity or gender—and they don't even try to understand things from the perspective of someone in your shoes, that could be a problem. For example, if you go to therapy because you're struggling with sexual harassment in the workplace and your male therapist tells you to simply "buck up," you're probably on the wrong couch.

I don't think I need to belabor the point here. I just want you to be aware that perspective matters. I'm not saying you always need to pick a therapist who is exactly like you. I'm just saying that you need to think about perspective during the process of choosing your person. Indeed, many times I think it is helpful to get assistance from someone with totally different life experiences. But that's just me.

Give yourself a gut check regularly

Therapy is a weird thing. Sometimes, you can show up to try to deal with one issue and find that you've got 57 other issues that you need to deal with first. That's a powerful road to walk with someone. Often, the very act of relieving yourself from these woes can feel so good that you lose sight of the original goal. That's ok.

Sometimes you start therapy without having a clue what your actual goal should be. That's ok too.

There is one thing, however, that I want you to remain cognizant of throughout your therapeutic process. Specifically, I want you to do a monthly check-in on those questions I set forth above. Because no matter what goals you and your practitioner set, I want you to keep *your ideal life* as one of your main goals. If you're not thinking about it, it won't happen. I fully believe in the age-old adage that "thoughts become things." It may not be healthy to obsess about your ideal life, but you should never, ever lose sight of it.

Also, I want you to do a monthly gut check on your relationship with your practitioner. Therapeutic abuse is rare, but it can happen. A good friend of mine was slowly and methodically seduced by her therapist. It seemed incredibly romantic at the time but looking back—some 10 years later—she can see that there was more manipulation than anything else. And it ended up being a pretty painful experience. She once told me that if she had ever just stepped away from the thrill of the romance for a second, her rational mind would have told her to run far and fast in the opposite direction.

That situation is definitely an anomaly. More commonly, if a therapist or counselor "fails," they may simply fail to move you toward your goals. They may be comforting to talk to or covered by your insurance or whatever, but if they're not moving you forward, what's the point? The problem is, it is so easy to get mired in the *process* of therapy that you forget to check in with yourself, by yourself.

Give it a try. I sincerely hope your gut tells you you're on the right track.

Your gut also knows when you need help

Remember three minutes ago when I asked you to trust your gut when it comes to assessing whether your practitioner is really good for you? I'm a big believer in the gut check. And I implore you to use it when you are considering whether you need to seek out the help of a professional in the first place.

Look, the very last thing I want to do with this chapter is dissuade anyone from seeking the help of a psychologist, psychiatrist, counselor, licensed clinical social worker, primary care physician, shaman, psychic, medium, or astrologer. If your gut or heart or mind or body or soul tells you that you need help, then run—don't walk—to the professional of your choice.

All I want you to do is be smart about it. Don't allow them to talk you out of being you. Don't let them make you believe you need their permission for anything. This life is yours for the taking! Go grab it!

"There is nothing stronger than a broken woman who has rebuilt herself."

—Hannah Gadsby

Eight

The "V" Word

You'll recall that way back in the Prologue I talked rather extensively about "my IT moment." If you're like some other people I know, you might make a habit of skipping the Prologue so you can get to the heart of the matter. You can't do that here . . . you have permission to go back and read it now because "my IT moment" was a major catalyst for my life transformation.

Other women, of course, have stories that are just as tragic. One woman I know was raped at the Naval Academy. When she complained to superior officers, she was kicked out of the Academy, her scholarship was revoked, and the military demanded that she return the scholarship dollars she had received prior to that point. That's when "it" happened to her.

And, like me, IT haunted her for years. She ended up marrying an abusive husband. He tortured her both psychologically and physically until she was just a shell of her former self. Despite her amazing credentials, she ended up barely scraping by for years as she wondered what the hell could have happened to the strong, break-neck woman she had been upon entering the Naval Academy.

Another friend of mine lost her dad, her sister, and her best friend in a span of six years. Cancer, suicide, cancer. As she was grieving, she connected with a partner who turned out to be a sociopath. You may be sensing (correctly) that that is not such an unusual course. As it turns out, once a person has experienced "it," they become susceptible to partnering with charlatans, thieves, and sociopaths—all of whom draw strength from the underlying weakness.

In my friend's case, it only took a few years until her bank accounts had been drained, this person was sleeping with the neighbor, and the neighbor and the sociopath later orchestrated a horrible crime against my friend. All of that caused her "it" to grow even larger.

Just by virtue of the fact that you're reading this book, I'm guessing "it" may have happened to you too at some point. I'm certain you know others that "it" has happened to.

The "it" I'm referring to is hard to describe without using the ever-unpopular "V" word. Put simply, "it" is the moment that your life—or your very identity—becomes defined by victimhood. It is when the thing (or things) that happened to you are so ingrained in your character that you cannot tell the story of you without starting and ending with the story of your tragedy.

Now, please hear me when I say this—I am not suggesting that I or any of the women I talked about above did anything wrong by becoming entrenched in our victimhood. That, I believe, is inescapable in many circumstances. It's what we do with our victimhood that ultimately matters.

Consequently, what I want to talk about in this chapter is how you can redefine yourself following one of these "it" episodes. How you can eventually become the victor instead of the victim. It is possible, you know. And guess what? It all starts with realizing you are bent, not broken.

Bent but not broken

There's a duet that P!nk sings with Nate Ruess called "Learn to love again." If you haven't heard it, I highly recommend it. (By the way, going to a P!nk concert was on my bucket list—done! It was amazing!) Anyway, there's a line within the chorus that says, "we're not broken, just bent, and we can learn to love again." No matter how mired you are in "it" right now, YOU need to remember that you're not broken, just bent. You don't need permission to get out of your victimhood—well, not from anyone but yourself that is.

Before we can even talk about healing, however, we have to come to terms about being bent. Because tragedies of the magnitude we're talking about here absolutely, positively beg us to knock us off our center. And guess what? It's ok if you are. In fact, it might be necessary for you to live in your uncomfortable "bentness," while you summon the courage to move forward.

Think about it for a minute. So, your husband dies in a freak airplane crash . . . your child devolves into a life of drugs and confusion . . . your spouse is convicted of murder. These are not normal things. You don't get to wake up the next morning and make coffee like normal, feed the kids like normal, go to work like normal, do laundry like normal, or do whatever "normal" looks like to you. Because, my dear, your normal has disappeared.

Instead, you get to sit and stare at a wall. Or drink too much vodka at breakfast. Or curl up in the fetal position on the bathroom floor while you cry and blow your nose in your shirt. You get a pass here. You, my sweet friend, have been handed a shit sandwich. You didn't order it, you don't like it, but there it is on your plate. Now what are you going to do with your shit sandwich?

There's only one thing I'm going to ask you to try desperately *not* to do. Please don't start blaming yourself. Please—and you won't hear me say this often—please allow yourself to simply be a victim. Hurt. Cry. Scream. Repeat. Don't go to work. Let somebody else take care of the kids for a while. Drink too much. Punch holes in the wall. You've earned all of these "unapproved behaviors" and I want you to exploit the hell out of them.

Why? Because if you don't do it now; if you act like everything is ok; if you get up and put on a strong face—all of this will explode out of you at some later date. I promise you that. And guess what? Six years from now, when you finally decide to be a mess, no one is going to understand what the hell is wrong with you.

They'll be actively forgetting your tragedy at the same time that your problem finally causes a bleeding ulcer, destroys your liver, causes a heart attack, or whatever malady your body comes up with to get you to stop. And when you break, they'll scoff. There will be no casseroles or invitations to "Netflix and chill" with your girls. You'll simply be "the crazy lady who had a nervous breakdown."

So now is your time. I'm sorry you're here. I'm sorry you're experiencing this. I remember how awful it was. But if I can make one wish for you in this time of tragedy, it is that you let yourself just be right in this moment. Go on, you can do it.

How the victim mindset takes hold

Believe it or not, that last section was easy to write. I fully believe that you need to give yourself time to find your center before you can mend. But there are traps associated with staying in that frame of mind too long. And let me just warn you in advance, this is not going to be an easy conversation between you and me. Why? Well, for one thing, I'm going to have to be brutally honest about prolonged victimhood. It ain't pretty. Let's walk through the steps.

First, of course, some external force breaks you. It can break your spirit, your mind, your body—or sometimes all three simultaneously. Your heartache quickly becomes the first thing you talk about to family, friends, and even strangers. You may even discuss your challenges on social media. "Victim" becomes your identity. As a result, you get a lot of sympathy and a lot of support (emotional, physical, and sometimes financial). People are tripping over themselves to take care of things for you. This is a time that you may experience true human compassion. That is a wonderful thing, isn't it?

Unwittingly, all of those people who are so sweetly supporting you may be doing you a disservice. Specifically, they may be unintentionally teaching you that victimhood is not a bad place to be. Your needs are taken care of. You have an excuse for not doing the things you should do. When you screw up, people are more forgiving than usual. It can actually feel pretty safe. If it weren't for the original tragedy, it would be kind of an idyllic life—almost like being part of the royal family. You have very little responsibility and everyone's ok with it.

Consequently, a person can get almost addicted to being a victim. After all, so long as we maintain that identity, we don't really have to do much. We can use our situation as an excuse for not performing at our best. Hell, we can use it as an excuse to stay in bed, gain weight, be grumpy, fail to pay our bills, let our appearance go, not keep in touch with people—you name it, we can make an excuse for it!

To make matters worse, being stuck in a mindset of victimhood tends to draw more instances of being a victim. Remember the friend I talked about above who got entangled with a sociopathic partner during a time when she was trying to regain her strength? As I said, that's not unusual.

Sadly, there are many sharks in the waters. When they smell you bleeding, they'll swim at you with lightning speed to take another bite out of your soul. And guess what? You'll let them. Wanna know why? Because victimhood has become your identity, your addiction, your best friend. As a result, you can easily let yourself be victimized over and over and over—all the while wondering, "why me?"

Not surprisingly, at some point we all realize this. We know it is time to move on and grow into our power, but we're still painfully unsure that we can face our old responsibilities. That fear grows and grows and grows at the same time that being a victim provides more and more comfort. We get stuck. And nothing could be more understandable than that.

But guess what, my friend? At some point, you've gotta get out of that rut. This tragedy was not the definition you had for your life—do not let it define you now. It would be very easy to stay right there and fade away. You deserve better. You have to get out of bed. Do the dishes. Eat a healthy meal. Pay those bills. Put that wine bottle down. Make and keep a date with a friend. Get dressed. Do your hair.

Be alive.

How the f* are you supposed to do that? We'll talk about it. But first there's one more elephant in the room that we need to discuss—shame.

The pit of shame

Victimhood has a very close cousin who is just as ugly, just as insidious, as victimhood itself. It's called shame and it is so closely tied to victimhood that it actually helps your victimhood hold you down. It doesn't matter exactly what happened to you that led to your break. Shame will grab hold and make you feel complicit—and incredibly guilty.

You know what I'm talking about, right? If your husband was killed in a car accident, shame tells you that if only you hadn't asked him to pick up milk on the way home, he'd be alive today. If you've contracted a horrible disease, shame tells you that it is your fault for living an unhealthy life. When my spouse committed murder (an act, by the way, that had absolutely, positively nothing to do with me), shame convinced me that if I had only been a more attentive partner, that horrible act never would have been committed.

And, of course, shame doesn't stop there. Shame makes you feel terrible for being a victim. It makes you hate the fact that you can't get out of bed some days, even though you were the type to rise and shine by 5 am for your entire life—until "it" happened. Shame tells you that you're fat and ugly, but also holds your hand while you order those chili cheese fries. Shame makes you unable to open the bills that come in the mail that you know you can't pay. Shame beats on you and beats on you and beats on you every second of every day.

In other words, my friend, you also become a victim of your own shame. Can you see now why victimhood is so hard to get out of?

All this to say, one of things you're going to have to do to get out of your victimhood is to overpower your shame. We'll talk more about how you can do that below. For now, simply trust me when I tell you that this is something you are absolutely capable of doing. And the first step is really identifying, acknowledging, and owning all of the ways that you are currently experiencing shame.

Find your tribe

One of the worst things about being the victim of an awful tragedy is that it can be terribly isolating. Once the well-intended casseroles stop coming to your door and the Hallmark cards stop arriving in your mailbox, you are alone. Even if you have children or a significant other, you're typically alone with your unique perspective on what has just happened to you.

It is a devastating, bone-chilling loneliness. It's more than just eating frozen dinners in your pajamas on a Friday night. It's the realization and belief that no one in the whole world understands what you've just gone through.

Aside from how sad this is, let's pause for a moment and realize just how dangerous this state of affairs can be. According to some sources, prolonged loneliness can make you 50% more likely to suffer premature death than your non-lonely peers. It is as bad for you as smoking nearly a pack of cigarettes a day. And the worst part is, your tragedy may very likely demand that you stay lonely for a significant period of time. You must fight this urge. Grab a pack of cigs and call some friends! (I am kidding, of course. If only it was that easy.)

At some point, you have to find your tribe. The good news is that there are a ton of resources out there for you. There are grief groups, sexual assault survivor groups, narcissist survivor groups, and on and on.

Name your tragedy and I'm willing to bet that there is a group out there just for you. Even if it is not located near you, you might find wonderful, thriving online communities where you can find other people who will relate to your situation. Even in my highly unique situation, there were groups I could reach out to: LOOPS (Loved Ones of Prisoners) and FamilyArrested.com are just two examples.

So, what does this tribe do for you? Well, for one thing, they normalize your experience. They give you other people to talk to who can truly understand what you've been through. They can offer tips for how you can start to live again, post-tragedy. And perhaps most importantly, they can help carry you from "victim" to "survivor"—which is a huge transition.

Now that I've got you all jazzed about joining a group, let me give you a word of caution. Do your research before you join anything. Some of these groups may be focused on keeping you (and them) mired in your victimhood. That's understandable but it's not for you. You're going to move on in life and you need strong people around you to do that. If you sense that a group is only about being down and out --and not about rising up—leave quickly.

While your new-found group is lifting you up, you can take this rare opportunity (rare means valuable, do not piss it away) to reinvent yourself as a badass. Yep, life is new. Everything before today sucked. I get it, but let's consider this moment as your refresh button. When you wake up tomorrow, you get to decide who you want to be, what you want to experience, and the gift you want to leave to this world. Because a lot of times, bullshit traumatic experiences are simply a wakeup call. A clarion to live your life to the fullest. Don't dismiss the call—run headfirst into it.

And if you need help figuring out what this new life looks like for you, continue on to the next chapter, where we'll help you find your Mission Essential (ME). I am watching you . . . let's see what you got, girl.

One other tip on finding your tribe—don't forget your BFFs. That sounds obvious, I know, but hear me out. Lots of times, when someone goes through a tragedy, they reject anyone and everyone who has not also been through that same daunting experience. Sometimes this is out of embarrassment or shame. Sometimes, it is just out of a desire to self-isolate. Regardless of the reason, I firmly believe that it is important to keep a touchstone—someone who knew you before the tragedy and who is willing to stand by your side afterwards. That person may get frustrated with you. They may get mad at you. But they will always keep you real. So hang on. My best friend did this for me and you may have to do it for your best friend someday. That is seriously the great thing about BFFs. You can lean on them. Hard.

One final note here before we move on from this idea of finding your tribe. Please always remember that there will come a day when you are better. You may not believe it right now, but it is true. What I'm asking of you in this moment is that you remain open to being in someone else's tribe when this whole mess is behind you. They're going to need you then as much as you need your mentors today. You don't have to make the decision right now. Just consider it.

Getting out of the black hole

If this chapter applies to you, I want you to know that I'm with you and I support you in your efforts to survive and thrive. I am super tempted to give you a list of tools that you can use in order to get better. But guess what? I already did.

Chapter 12 is called "Innate Supreme Wisdom." It's going to walk you through the vast array of healing tools that are available to you right now, today (and many without costing you a dime). Pay particular attention to the ideas surrounding neuroplasticity. This is going to be a critical tool for you to use once you decide to overcome your shame and your victimhood. Also reread Chapter 7 (*Hiring So-Called Pros*) regarding how you can find (and keep) qualified mental health professionals. Redo the exercises in that chapter. Focus on your healing and on your ultimate desire to get out of this hole.

Along the way, give yourself goals. Celebrate—I mean *really* celebrate—when you reach them. Acknowledge your strength and growth through every step. And look, I'm here to tell you that things that are *major* victories to you might seem minor to someone else. Maybe it is as simple as paying a bill on time. Or getting out and walking for 15 minutes. Or sleeping through the night. No one else needs to understand how big those hurdles are for you. Do NOT be ashamed that your victories are small compared to someone else's. You need to acknowledge and celebrate every single one.

I totally understand how easy it is to stay in that dark place; to keep licking wounds long after they have scarred over. I know how hard it is to single handedly turn that massive dark force around. But you must. For yourself, for all that you are in this lifetime, it is the most important thing you can do for yourself.

You have permission!

What are you waiting for? I will be here, cheering you on.

"Your life is the sum result of all the choices you make, both consciously and unconsciously. If you can control the process of choosing, you can take control of all aspects of your life.
You can find the freedom that comes from being in charge of yourself."

—Robert F. Bennett

Nine

Your Mission Essential (ME)

What is your Mission Essential (ME)?

Let me cut right to the chase. In asking that question, I'm trying to understand what your essential purpose in life is. Why are you here? What emotions drive how you live your life? What do you hope to accomplish during your time on this planet? What motto guides the actions you take day in and day out?

If you're like most people, your immediate answer will come in one of two forms:

"WTF are you talking about?" Or . . .

"My purpose in life is to serve God, family, and community."

If you fall in the first category, read on. If you're in the second, <u>stop it!</u> This isn't about what you do for other people or deities. Finding your Mission Essential (ME) is about finding your *internal* motivators that move you through the world.

It sounds like a simple concept but honestly, people screw it up all the time. Of course, you could just choose to ignore the whole concept. We all know life is infinitely easier when we bury our heads in the sand.

In the event you're willing to traverse this journey with me, let me give you an example that illustrates my point. Specifically, I want to examine one of the "purpose statements" I hear from my coaching clients all the time—"My essential purpose in life is to make money."

Nope, sorry. That is not a Mission Essential (ME) statement. It may be a *goal*, but it is not your *mission*. Why? Because money is an *external* factor. Your Mission Essential (ME) statement should be more closely aligned to the emotional driver behind your desire to make money. Try these variations on for size:

"My purpose is to live a life without fearing that I will die poor and scared."

"My purpose in life is to have the freedom to travel wherever I want, whenever I want."

Living out either of those statements will necessarily require a degree of financial security. But they are more intrinsically connected to your emotions than a simple drive toward the almighty dollar. Your mission statement is a reflection of those deep-rooted emotions.

For example, maybe your desire to live without fear comes from growing up in poverty. Perhaps you watched your parents struggle just to keep food on the table and you never want to be in a similar position.

Others may be hyper-aware of the constricting expectations of life and just want to be free to live on their own terms in a spectacular, beautiful place. Those are real, tangible, emotional things that could impact how you move through life. Finding your Mission Essential (ME) requires a deep, intentional focus on who you are, where you've been, and how you want to continue showing up in this world—in other words, your ME is your core internal compass.

Ready to get started on finding your ME? Not so fast, Sparky.

Getting ok with being selfish—and understanding what selfish means

Without a doubt, Friedrich Wilhelm Nietzsche (1844–1900) was one of the great thinkers on the topic of selfishness—a trait he viewed as a necessary virtue.

According to Nietzsche, living a *selfless* life was the easy, cowardly way to live. On the other hand, living according to one's own needs and desires, unrestrained from conformity and bound only to one's own creative spirit—that was living boldly and authentically. And guess what? I firmly believe he was right.

Think about it for a moment. When you aspire to live a selfless life, you necessarily take on the beliefs, victories, and burdens of others. Once that occurs, what happens to you? Your own burdens? You and they become buried in conformity. Does that make you happy? I'm guessing not. The remedy for that unhappiness lies in selfishness.

And so, before we get your ME nailed down, I'm going to have to drill a very important concept into your head—in finding your ME, you must be unabashedly selfish. I know that everything you've been taught up to this point has led you to believe that being selfish is a bad thing. That is most definitely not true. In fact, I believe that living a purposeful life demands a large degree of *healthy* selfishness.

To illustrate this point, I want you to think about firefighters for a minute. Why firefighters? Because they are some of the most **selfish** people on the planet. I can hear your disdain for that statement as I type. You probably believe firefighters are among the most self*less* beings around. Not so. Let me explain.

Most of us have known a firefighter or two in our lives. They're good people. They dedicate themselves to helping others who are in dire situations every single day. Even outside of work, they tend to be the people who help neighbors with yard projects, lend tools to friends, and volunteer for community events.

In fact, most firefighters think of themselves as superheroes. That is why they do all the things we've just discussed. They are constantly creating a story that fits their vision of a superhero—because that is their ME. They reinforce that story over and over and over in their lives. Don't believe me? Consider this:

Depending on where you live, firefighters earn between $50,000 to $75,000 per year. That is not a lot of money in today's economy. Nonetheless, every time someone's house catches fire, those brave women and men are running into the blaze while the weary victims are running out.

Clearly, these folks are not risking death and injury for $50,000 a year. Why would they when they could easily earn that amount (and more) as a construction worker, project manager, or accountant? They do it because every time they run into a burning structure; they are reinforcing their superhero image. We don't think of them as selfish, but they actually are. They are serving their Mission Essential in every dangerous situation.

Before you start to send me hate mail, remember that like Nietzsche, I don't believe selfishness is a bad thing. Selfishness, in fact, is a critical factor in helping us live our lives with purpose. Maybe you're still not convinced. After all, firefighters are an extreme example. That's fine. We can look at something a little more common.

I'm guessing that many of my readers are parents. If so, think back to the first several months after your oldest child was born. Those little suckers take so much work. That first baby can destroy your sleep patterns, your finances, your sex life, and your relationship. Every time they make a peep, you run to them. You can't even enjoy a few hours away from home without worrying for their safety. If we're going to be honest about first-born babies, they are the greatest burden many of us will ever know.

So, after living through all the hassle and drama of a first child's first year, why in the world do any of us ever have more children? When I ask my clients this question, I almost always get the same answer: "Because my children give me more than I give them."

Think about that for a minute.

As a species, we breed repeatedly because our children give us more than we give them. Guess what? That's **selfish**. We may not love the sleepless nights, the endless diapers, the crying, the messes, the noise, the interruption to our relationships—but we keep having them because they give us more than we give them. Pure selfishness!

Not a parent? That's okay. I have an example for you as well. Let's say that you simply have healthy boundaries in your relationships. Maybe when you start dating someone seriously, you demand that you get to spend every Sunday morning reading the New York Times alone.

No matter what else is going on, your partner knows that you're going to need four hours each Sunday to yourself. Sounds lovely, right? You may even be saying, "Huh! Must be nice!" It is, but it's also selfish! If you wish you could do this and are not . . . Isn't it about time you gave yourself permission to do the things that make you (and you alone) happy? It is a very healthy form of selfishness.

Maybe reading the Sunday paper from cover to cover makes you feel more informed about worldly affairs. Maybe it helps you at work to have a well-rounded understanding of current events. Both of those motivations are selfish—and they are also awesome.

And remember, there's no judgment here when it comes to selfishness. Sometimes—many times, in fact—selfishness is hard-wired in our brains. In fact, our biology often dictates that we act selfishly. Do you ever demand alone time so you can play the ukulele, write poetry, or build a sculpture? NO?!? You should . . .

In fact, evolutionary biologists would tell us that we likely do those things based on an innate desire to be more accepted socially or to be more attractive to potential mates. Both of those outcomes, in turn, make it more likely that we'll get a chance to pass our genes on to future generations. In other words, our biological drive to procreate can lead us down all sorts of selfish paths. How wonderful!

It may seem ridiculous to consider such trivialities as selfish, but they actually are. If you were acting selflessly, you would forgo your creative time in order to be of service to others. Most of us don't, however, because our biological selfishness dictates our behavior. What I'm advocating for in this chapter is that when it comes to defining your Mission Essential, you allow your emotional (and biological) selfishness to take center stage.

So, are you ready to find your ME? Put on your selfish hat and let's go.

What finding your Mission Essential (ME) looks like

One of the most rewarding aspects of my coaching career is putting people through the utter discomfort of finding their ME. Almost without fail, my clients—many of whom would likely describe themselves as the "tough guys" of the business world—end up in tears during this process. You may be thinking that if I like that, I'm some sort of masochist. That may be a fair assessment, if not totally accurate. If I'm honest, I realize that when I make grown men and women cry, I know we have hit the emotional well that will allow them to live the very best lives that they can. And I have to say, I selfishly like that.

What I love is that after my clients do the deep, harrowing, emotional work that it takes to define their ME, they almost always go on to lead healthier, happier, more successful lives.

By defining their Mission Essential, every decision they make from that day forward can be guided by whether or not they're staying on-purpose. Let me give you a couple of examples:

A warm cup of tea on a Sunday afternoon

One of my clients is a business run by a husband and wife team. When the couple first came to me, they were in that empty-nester phase of life. Their children were grown, had left the house, and suddenly the wife was struggling to find purpose.

She had been principally responsible for raising the couple's children even though she also worked in the business for all those years. After the kids left and her role in the business became more substantial, she was struggling to define her place in this new reality.

When we first spoke, this woman expressed a degree of complacency about the process. That, to me, is unacceptable. I told her that if she wanted to maintain the status quo, I had no interest in working with their business. My job is to lift people, not to help them remain static. I challenged her by putting through the rigorous process of finding her Mission Essential. You know what she came up with? "A warm cup of tea on a Sunday afternoon."

Fortunately, she allowed me to explore this concept with her a little more. For her, a warm cup of tea on a Sunday afternoon represented caring, nurturing, a warm hug. She had been that for her children for all of those years. It was her role and she loved it. It made her feel needed.

Now that she was more firmly entrenched in the business, that warm cup of tea actually remained her Mission Essential. Why? Because suddenly she was bringing that intense level of care and nurturing to the management team. And guess what? They were thriving because of it. During all those years when her husband was the head honcho, he managed with an iron fist. When she came into the business full-time, she brought her cup of tea with her. She brought nurturing, compassion, listening skills, and warmth.

That was her comfort place, whether it was aimed at her children or her employees. And, although you may think her purpose was ultimately to serve others, you're wrong. Her purpose was the sense of satisfaction *she* gained when others flourished under her care. Selfish! And awesome.

I'm not the sailor, I'm the pirate

Another client of mine was also struggling to come up with his Mission Essential. As I do with most clients, I put him through my proprietary process for defining one's own ME (you'll get a chance to go through this test for yourself at the end of the chapter).

After some intense sessions, here's what he came up with: "I'm not the sailor, I'm the pirate."

What this meant for him was that he was happiest in life when he was breaking things apart and putting them back together. He didn't put them back together in their original form, however. When this guy put something back together, he made whatever machine he was working on *better than it was before.* In other words, he was never an obedient sailor who did as he was told. Rather, he was the pirate who consistently sought to do things differently—and always better.

Once he realized this Mission Essential, he went on to revolutionize an entire industry—the funeral industry of all things. Looking at the funeral business from the standpoint of the sailor, a funeral was supposed to involve a somber speech, perhaps a viewing of the body, orchestral music, and lots and lots of crying. When he looked at that same business from the standpoint of the pirate, on the other hand, he saw it very differently.

People show up to funerals in order to honor the dead. They can either be relentlessly sad for a few hours or, guess what? They can celebrate! After defining his ME, my client came up with a video service that aims to bring people back to life during the service. That way, attendees can laugh with the deceased and experience their true spirit one more time before saying goodbye. What a beautiful outcome for a pirate to have concocted.

Go big or go home!

Given all the work I've done with others around finding their Mission Essential, you may be wondering what my ME is. If you're the type of person to pay attention to subheadings, you just read it: "Go big or go home."

When I went through the process, I was having a hard time coming up with my final "bumper sticker" to represent my ME. It haunted me for weeks. I knew the essence of it, but I needed a memorable short tag line for who I am. My youngest daughter identified it for me when she was around 11 years old. She noticed that in everything I did, I did it with gusto.

She was right. Every time I take on a new project, interest, or business endeavor, I'm either going to give it everything I've got and see it through to completion, or I'm not going to do it at all. I disdain mediocrity . . . 50% grey . . . blahhhhh. I know that if I am put in that situation, I cannot flourish, as matter of fact I self-implode.

That mission—"Go big or go home"—informs every single thing I do in life (even writing this book). If I can't envision it bigger, if I can't do it and do it with impact, I'm simply not going to start. So, when faced with any new challenge or opportunity, I ask myself, "can I give this everything I've got, can I make a huge impact with this?" If the answer is yes, I proceed, if the answer is no, I walk away. It's that simple.

I should also note that this is a purely selfish drive on my part. My time is much too valuable to spend on something that does not completely light me up. Therefore, if I'm not going to achieve that feeling, whatever the project is, it simply isn't worth my time.

The beauty in having a compass

Ultimately, the true joy in defining your Mission Essential (ME) is that you now have a compass that can guide you through everything in your life. To me, a person without a defined purpose is like a ship sailing at sea without any navigational tools whatsoever. That ship is simply adrift. It may land in a safe place and it may land in harm's way. One thing is for certain, however . . . the captain of the ship has no say in the matter.

Until you define your Mission Essential, you're exactly like that ship's captain. Life may bring you abundance, happiness, money, healthy relationships, and general well-being. Or, it can bring you consternation, grief, hardship, and chaos. Once you realize the crapshoot that is life without a Mission Essential, why in the world would you do anything at all in this moment except try to define your ME? Ready to get started? I thought so.

In the next section, I'm going to present you with the actual written questions that I provide to my clients when they agree to let me help them find their Mission Essential. Now, understand that in real life (outside of this book), I spend weeks with each client cultivating the ideas they've expressed in order to come up with a life-defining ME. Obviously, we can't do that here (because my "Go big or go home" ME tells me that this book will sell millions of copies and I simply won't have the time I would want to give each of you . . . the clock is ticking!).

Don't despair! You'll get a significant start just by going through these questions by yourself. The key is to be completely honest, authentic, and patient with yourself as you go through the process. Have fun and remember, this is all about you—you really can't screw it up.

Finding your Mission Essential

Our Mission Essential is "ground zero." It's the place from which all of your decisions should be made—big and small. When you're living life from an intentional place, you have some measure of control over how aligned your actions and outcomes are with your Mission. That alignment with your personal values, your passions, and your entire reason for being puts you on the path to a life well-lived. What could be more important and rewarding than living a life that made a difference . . . however you define that difference?

The answers you come to in this exercise will be useful to you if (and *only* if) you answer them honestly. Therefore, the two rules for this exercise are:

1. You must answer each question with depth. If you are tempted to "phone it in" and give half-answers, don't waste your time.

2. You must answer these questions from your heart.

The answers can't just represent what you think you should say, based on other people's judgements or expectations. If you need to keep it completely confidential so that you can answer them with total honesty, then do that.

These are basic questions to seed the full narrative. Consider them to be the minimum information you need to develop your Mission Essential, but also feel free to add more detail to make this exercise your own.

1. Seeding questions—to get you thinking and feeling

The following list of questions is designed to stimulate your thoughts and put you in the right frame of mind for working on your ME.

Be mindful about your answers. There are no right or wrong answers—just answers that are true for you. Some questions have easy, obvious answers; some questions have difficult answers that require a great deal of thought; and some questions might cause you to rethink some of your most basic values and attitudes. Remember— most importantly, be honest with yourself as you reflect on, and then answer these questions. Push yourself to go a little deeper with your thinking. It is meant to make you uncomfortable.

What do you value most? What's especially important to you?

What matters most at this point in your life? Has that changed recently, or do you think it should change from this point forward?

What will be your legacy? (A way to think about "legacy" might be: The path you forge for those who come after you. The "breadcrumbs" you leave behind to provide guidance, direction, or means to live a better life than if they'd not been given that gift. Or very simply, it might even mean an inheritance).

What would you like people's perceptions of you to be?

What do you daydream about?

At 2:00 AM when you can't get back to sleep, where does your mind go?

Of all the things you've done in your life so far, what has given you the most satisfaction or pleasure?

When you were little—say, between 7-14 years old, what did you want to be?

If you no longer had to work, how would you spend your time, and with whom? Why them?

What motivates you to exceed others' expectations?

What are your greatest strengths?

What are your greatest weaknesses?

2. What don't you want in your life?

Now, list anything that comes up that causes you anger, stress, frustration, fear, hatred, embarrassment, dissatisfaction—and anything else that you do not want in your life. Don't think too much, just write as many as you can think of—You will clean this list up later . . .

Good! Now, take a deep breath. Some of this isn't easy to confront when approached with this level of self-honesty.

While you're in the zone, now try to prioritize the list above. Include between five to seven factors that you find to be the most important to not have in your life.

3. What do you want in your life?

At the bottom of the page you've been working on, list everything that you do want in your life. If you get stuck, try to contrast with what you don't want above. This is a bit of a shift here, given what you just focused on. So, try to mentally and emotionally imagine those things that make you feel blissful, fulfilled, satisfied, and what energizes you. Material or intrinsic; shallow or deep—Whatever comes to your head and heart. Again, don't think too much about it, and write as many as you can.

Hopefully, that was more pleasant. Now, again, while you're in the zone here, try to find patterns and focus on the ones that have real depth. If there are material things on the list above, no worries. What do they represent that's more substantial? Try to limit this to about five to seven of the most significant things that bring you deep joy.

4. Death & taxes

As they say, "No one gets out of here alive." Ultimately, we will all come to the same fate. We've got a finite number of days on this planet, and as far as we know, this is our only shot to do it right.

So, what does "right" look like for you? What will your most special loved ones say about you when you've gone? Yes, this is a very sobering exercise. But we really try to lean into the hard and difficult things here, so let's dive right in . . .

Write an obituary, eulogy, or posthumous tribute to honor the life that you will have lived.

5. Who are you?

A summary statement which I like to call your "bumper sticker" is useful at this point. Declaring your Mission Essential is a way to bring these words into something that represents your guiding principles. The decisions you make—big and small—are to be vetted against this standard for conduct, purpose, and values.

Ideally, you will have come to a pithy saying that means absolutely nothing to anyone else. Remember . . . "I am not the sailor, I am the pirate" or "Go big or go home" or "I am a warm cup of tea on a Sunday afternoon." But for you it is an emotional power pack for all your future endeavors. Look for patterns . . . ask yourself "why" at least 5 times . . . don't be afraid to dig. Then and only then will you begin to see the essence that is you.

You got this! I'm guessing you will be pleasantly surprised with the outcome.

Wrap up

Wait! What?!? You have read through the questions without actually putting pen to paper? Why? Do you not feel worthy? It is a waste of your time? You feel selfish? All garbage thinking.

Let's try this again. This exercise works best when your thoughts and responses are immediate and gut-level. The good news is, it's not too late. Go back right now and actually respond to the questions I've posed.

Look, I know this is not an easy process. It may make you want to scream, kick things, and generally engage in destructive behavior. Don't succumb to the madness. No matter how many tears you shed in this process, the end result will be incredibly valuable to every single day you have remaining on this planet. As we discussed in earlier chapters, none of us knows how many days we have left. Why not make the best of each and every one of them?

Go ahead. Get started. What's your Mission Essential?

"Whenever you find yourself on the side of
the majority, it is time to reform
(or pause and reflect)."

—Mark Twain

Ten

Be Bold

So, you've defined your Mission Essential—congratulations! And, if you haven't, WTF? Go back to Chapter 9 and do that now. You'll need your ME in order to move on to this next concept.

You're back! Great! Now I want you to stop everything you're doing (hopefully reading with rapt attention). If the TV is on, turn it off. Same with the radio. If the kids are screaming, try to get away from them for a minute (if they're under 10 years old, maybe have someone watch them—and don't worry, this won't take long).

Are you by yourself? Great. Now, grab a piece of paper and a pen. Here we go.

In the next 30 seconds, I want you to write a list of three to five personal values that guide you through your life. No questions, no excuses. Just write down your primary personal values.

. . .

So, what'd you come up with? Were you able to do it? I have so consciously lived my own personal values that when I was talking about this chapter with a friend recently, I was shocked to hear that she couldn't rattle off her own list from the cuff.

I thought at first that she had a major character flaw. Then we talked it through for a bit and I realized that not everyone keeps this list. That, in my humble opinion, is a huge mistake. But don't worry . . . we can correct it.

The importance of truly personal, personal values

It doesn't matter who you are, where you were brought up, or who raised you—you were gifted a set of personal values. Maybe you grew up in the foster care system and learned to be independent and self-sufficient. Those are values. Or, perhaps you were raised in a midwestern Christian family and were handed a set of values from your family and your church. The same goes for people raised by atheists, Republicans, Democrats, Libertarians, agnostics, schoolteachers, lawyers, doctors, construction workers, or any other title you can think of for the people who shaped your life. Whoever they were and whatever they believed in; they shared their values with you.

Culture also adds to our value system. Media figures, politicians, writers, artists, musicians . . . all of them share their values with the world. And, undoubtedly, some of those sink in over time.

A person who grew up in America, for example, might have very different cultural values from someone brought up in Brazil or the Netherlands or Tanzania or any other place. Heck, a person raised in California was likely exposed to a different set of values from someone raised in Texas or Maine.

All of those things are important. All are certainly influencers in your life. But, as you might suspect by now, I'm not talking about them. I don't particularly care about their values. We're here today, working our way through this book together, to talk about *your values*.

And guess what? It's ok if some of the values that were given to you as a child continue to guide your life to this day. It's also ok if they don't. What *is* important is that you give some long, hard thought to the three to five values that you want to shape your life—and then that you BE BOLD in living out those values.

Hence, the title of this chapter. I want you to Be Bold in whatever value system you value most. Why? Because until you decide to Be Bold in that precise manner, you are not living your best life. You are, as Mark Twain warned at the beginning of this chapter, simply part of the majority. That means it is time for you to stop and reflect. Is that where you truly belong?

Let's go back for a moment and consider those values that were gifted to you. The ones you learned from your family, your community, your religion, etc. Those are really easy to adopt (or, for some people, really easy to reject). But when your entire value system is based upon what someone else said, you're living a life of mediocrity. You're not forcing yourself to be your best you. You're simply doing what someone else before you did, without the autonomy of thought.

The friend I talked about earlier in this chapter . . . she theorizes that most people do not have clearly defined personal values. It's her bet that most of you, in fact, were not able to come up with a list of truly personal, personal values in the 30 seconds that I gave you.

That scares me. It not only scares me that we all might live in a world where we're not guided by strong personal values . . . It also scares me that so many people are living a life of mediocrity, or worse, are lambs being led to slaughter. Yeah, I get it, that is pretty dramatic. But if you are not leading your life, then someone else is. Are you sure you want to unconsciously give up that much control?

Here's what happens when you don't live your own personal values: you live a life of "shoulds." When faced with any situation, you decide what to do based on what those around you think you should do. You also judge others based on what your group-defined-values tell you they should or should not do. The larger the group, the more swift and strong the judgement will likely be. In this chapter, I'm inviting you to define your very own personal values so you can give yourself permission to live a life that is truly meaningful to you.

Nature vs. nurture

Before we get into the exercises where you will extract your own personal values, I want to spend a few minutes talking about the impacts of nature and nurture on your value system. The best way for me to do that is to continue talking, okay . . . bragging, about my two daughters.

As someone who relied on a clearly-defined value system, you better believe I was dead-set on imparting certain values to my two daughters. I wanted to be focused and pick the values that I thought were most important to help inform their lives more than anything else: (1) independence; and (2) think for yourself and you will always have choices. I'm sure I subtly passed on some of my other values along the way, but those were the two that I tried to drive home specifically.

It's not just that I wanted them to be independent. It's that I always wanted them to make choices based on their own individual beliefs, rather than basing those choices on what someone else thought was right.

Today, my girls are both in their twenties. As I was writing this chapter, I decided to text each of them and give them an impromptu quiz, by asking what their personal values are. The responses were fascinating.

Syd, my youngest, responded first, "Independence, intuition, drive, passion, competence." I proudly noted that she had claimed one of the two values I had hoped she would adopt.

Her older sister, Taylor, responded a short time later. Her list of values made me equally proud: "honesty, be kind no matter what, work hard, making time for people I love, healthy living, being in charge of your own life, and knowing you always have a choice."

Ultimately, both of the core values I tried to pass to my girls landed. I'm thrilled to share that with you. The interesting part was how they took the values I had instilled in them and added their own spin to it. It is fascinating to me how each one took a value that they had gotten from me and by combining their values with it, made up who they are as they are living BOLDLY!

Let me share a story about my oldest daughter.

Taylor's version of independence and think for yourself

When my girls were little, I tried to encourage them to participate in sports. I had been an athlete for most of my life and I believed that athletics would provide them with some strong lessons society might shortchange them on as women (drive, competition, strength, just to name a few). Consequently, almost as soon as Taylor was able to walk and run, I had her in a soccer league.

It was her third year in soccer at a time when she was well aware of the rules, the competitive game plan, and the expectations that she had on her as a player. But my daughter, being the one who was always aware of her choices, was not to be boxed into one way of thinking.

It was a close game with a neighborhood rival. Taylor was playing offense so she was hanging back in the field as the defense was defending her goal. Finally, the ball got taken away from the opponent and kicked out of the scrum, directly to Taylor. This was her big chance that she had worked so hard for and waited so patiently to materialize. Here was her moment, just her, the ball and nothing but open field between her and the other team's goal. She took control of the ball as it was passed out to her, spun around and began running down the field dribbling the ball to a certain goal. The crowd was going wild, the coach was swinging his arms and yelling "go, go, go!"

I was beaming as I watched my daughter work the ball down field. She had one opponent who was running as fast as she could to catch up to Taylor but Taylor was holding the lead. The goal was all but a sure thing until . . . the girl that was right on Taylor's tail, yelled up to Taylor, "My shoe is untied!" Taylor immediately stopped the soccer ball under her foot, turned around and looked at her competitor. The other girl kneeled down, tied her shoe, and then jumped up and said "Okay!" They both took off again running toward the goal! I saw parents grabbing their heads and yelling "NOOOOOO!" The coach was paralyzed and speechless all at once. Did Taylor make her shot?

It doesn't matter. My daughter knew in that moment that she could be independent and make her own choices. To my great pride, her choice was to be kind to a fellow soccer player. Honestly, I believe that moment defined who she is to this day. My heart exploded out of my chest. No, she wouldn't be a professional soccer player, or a good little soldier . . . but she ended up being so much more.

I'm extremely proud to be able to tell you that both my girls took my values, incorporated them into their lives, and made them their own. I wish I could take all the credit, but these primary values seem too innately ingrained in each of them for me to take the victory lap I want to take.

I tell you all this to emphasize my main point about your personal values—they may come from a variety of places. What is important right here and right now is that you recognize them, embrace them as uniquely yours (even if they came, in part, from someone else), and that you go forward and BE BOLD with them.

When your personal values are really going to matter

Before we get too far down the road to you knowing, living, and Being Bold with your truly personal, personal values, I want to be crystal clear on what this is going to do for you (and what it is not).

First of all, knowing and living your personal values is not necessarily going to make you into a better person—or even a happier person. You can be 100% connected to your personal values and still be miserable. Case in point: Adolf Hitler.

Perhaps at no time in history has one person been more clear on his personal values. And, without a doubt, that son of a bitch was incredibly bold with his. Hell, millions of people died and an entire World War raged for around six years because he was so convinced that propagation of a "pure" white race was the most important thing on the planet. One could argue that Hitler was the master of knowing his personal values, living them, and being exceptionally bold with them.

Fortunately, it is unlikely that anyone reading this book is a human monster like he was. Nonetheless, being connected with your personal values is not, as I've said, a guaranteed road to happiness. In fact, despite my deep connection to my own personal values, I've been through some incredibly dark and difficult times in my life (remember "my IT moment"?). And guess what? Even though my personal values didn't save me from that, they did help me survive and thrive. And that's the point. Read the following italicized text very carefully. Then stop, think about it, and read it again:

From time to time, life is going to kick your ass. It will throw you completely off-center. It is in those times, my friends, that you must be aware of your personal values—because they are the one thing that will bring you back to center.

I don't need to tell you about the millions of different ways that life can knock you sideways. Divorce, death of a loved one, serious illness, violent crime, emotional abuse. If I had to wager, I'd bet that 98% of the women reading this book have experienced one or more of those things. If you're one of them, you know that those experiences took you far afield from your sense of self.

So what if, in those times, you had something that could pull you back? Something that didn't necessarily take the pain away but did get you back on the road to healing? Something that allowed you to live your best life, despite the obstacles? You do! Your personal values. I want to share with you how one of my clients went through a life-altering situation and used her personal values to get back on track.

Stacy's story

When I first met Stacy, she had just become an empty-nester. Her entire life had been wrapped up in being a stay-at-home mom, caring for her kids, and making sure they had the very best life possible. When her youngest finally left for college, she was in the throes of depression and a complete identity crisis.

As we talked about her struggles, I asked her to list her personal values. I knew (even though she did not) that they were the key to getting her back on track. But, guess what? She couldn't list them. Sigh . . . we had to go deeper.

After much conversation, I got Stacy to explain what it was that she had loved so very much about being a mom. The first thing she talked about was the parties. She loved Christmas, birthday parties, weddings, and family get-togethers. She thrived off of the joy she could bring to a group of people (her family and friends), even if it was just for a few hours at a time. I could tell from her voice that this was something very deep and meaningful for her.

So, (surprise!) we went deeper. I asked her to think about what values she could extract from her experiences with family get togethers. She thought about it for a while and you know what she came up with? Fairy tales. Her whole life as a mom had been focused on allowing her children (and others in their lives) to experience pure happiness—one gathering at a time. She said she felt like there was so much strife in the world that creating a "fairy tale" was one of the greatest gifts she could give. But now her children were grown and gone and she felt like the fairy tales were gone with them. Nonsense!

This, for Stacy, was life's way of throwing her off-center. Luckily, I knew just what to do. I talked to Stacy about how she might be able to use her deep love of "fairy tales" in this new chapter in her life. It didn't take her long to respond—she could create an organization that gave those fairy tale moments for kids who didn't grow up in her family! In fact, she could gift those experiences to kids living in much worse circumstances.

Eureka! We had found a personal value that was core to Stacy's being. We found a way for her to live it, despite the changed circumstances in her life. Now all we had to do was get her to Be Bold with it.

"So," I asked her, "What's holding you back? Why not start working on this organization today?"

Her excuses were long and, frankly, boring. Mainly, she focused on the fact that she and her husband had moved to a new house in the past year, there were still boxes to unpack, and she was feeling like all of that was too physically demanding to tackle.

"Hire someone," I said, knowing she and her husband could afford it. "Hire someone to unpack all your stuff and YOU start worrying about creating fairy tales for the people who need you."

In other words, I gave her permission to move forward and Be Bold with her personal values. She didn't need my permission, but she also didn't know that yet. Fortunately, she took my advice and is thriving in her new business. She has a new sense of purpose that is completely in line with her values and is back to living her best life, notwithstanding the fact that her children are gone.

I turned to Stacy's example precisely because it is so sweet. Your situation may be more dire. Perhaps you have just lived through a serious illness. Maybe a spouse cheated on you and you're single for the first time in 20 years. Whatever it is, I promise you that if you do three things, your road to personal fulfillment will be much shorter and, well, much more fulfilling:

Define your personal values.

Live them.

BE BOLD with them.

Fortunately, the next section is going to help you do all of that. Ready to get started? Let's get on to that, shall we?

Defining your personal values

If, at the outset of this chapter, you were 100% able to list your core personal values in 30 seconds or less, right on, sister! That does not mean, however, that you get to skip this section. I invite you (nay, command you) to still go through the following exercises to see: (a) if your personal values are truly your personal values; (b) if there are values behind the values you listed (we want to break things down to their core); and (c) if you are actually being BOLD with respect to those values.

As we do this, I'm going to rely from time to time on the conversation I had with my friend who was unable to come up with her own list of values on the fly. It didn't take too long to get to the core of her values and I don't think it will take you too long either. Note: I said it didn't take long, I didn't say it was easy. With that in mind, let's dive in.

Exercise #1: Think of real-life scenarios that exemplify your values

A few minutes after I asked my friend (let's call her Joan) to define her values, our conversation took this turn:

Joan: "I don't think I can give you a list of my personal values, but I can give you an example of a situation where I had to use them."

Me: "I'm all ears."

Joan: "Ok, so several years ago, I was taking a late-night stroll with my partner through downtown Portland. It was the middle of winter and it was really cold. We were almost back to my place when we came across a homeless man on the side of the street. He was clearly having some sort of medical event . . . maybe a seizure, maybe something else. It was dark and it was hard to tell exactly what the problem was. My first instinct was to stop and help the guy. My partner was worried about stopping to talk to some strange man late at night but there was no way I was going to just walk by him. I didn't have my phone on me but after talking to him, it became clear that he needed help. I got him safely down on the sidewalk, covered him with my coat, and ran back to my apartment to get my phone so I could call 9-1-1. Then I ran back outside and waited with him until the paramedics came. So, I guess you could say one of my core values is compassion and helping people in need."

Me: "Ok, and what did your partner end up doing?"

Joan: "She thought I was crazy, begged me not to go back out to him, and generally dissuaded me from getting involved. To me, not helping wasn't an option. But I would say that's an innate drive in me. I never stopped to say, 'ok, my values tell me I should help this guy, so I will.' So, is that a value, or is that just a part of who I am?"

Me: "What do you think?"

Joan: "I think it's a value, but I don't think I needed to define it."

In this instance, Joan was partly right and partly wrong. She's right in that compassion/helping others is a core value of hers. But as we talked it through more, I learned that she probably isn't Being Bold with respect to her values. We'll return to that later.

For now, I challenge you to think of situations in your life where you, like Joan, took action without thinking. Obviously, I want you to recall scenarios where those actions seem to be aligned with what you suspect may be your core values.

What are you waiting for? Do that now!

Do you have an example (or, better yet, multiple examples)? Good. Now I want you to spend some time with them. What values come from those examples? Where do you think you got those values? Do they come from a sense of should? If so, I want you to discard them and start over.

Think of examples of situations where your truly personal, personal values caused you to act. Again, it's ok if you learned these values from someone else (Joan later explained that she learned to have compassion from her father). The most important thing is that you have consciously adopted the value as your very own, regardless of someone else's influence.

Exercise #2: Explore the values behind your character traits

Ok, so I've bagged on Joan enough for now. She's not the only person I've talked to who doesn't have a defined list of truly personal, personal values that she carries through life. I also spoke with a client recently (we'll call her Sarah) who didn't have a defined list of personal values. Not only that, she had a hard time coming up with anything that resembled a value. There was work to be done.

My first challenge to Sarah was to ask her to define some of her core characteristics.

"I'm an introvert," she said. "I realize that's not a value, but it really influences how I live in the world."

Never one to back down from a challenge, I asked Sarah why she was an introvert. I knew there had to be a value system in there somewhere.

"Well," she said, "I was brought up to believe you should only speak when spoken to. That you should never interrupt. That you should be seen and not heard. I guess to the extent I carry those things forward in my adulthood, they are values."

"Wrong," I told her. We dug deeper.

Ultimately, those childhood messages had nothing to do with Sarah's value system. What she did value in life were things like safety, comfort, and security. When she would go to parties with hoards of people she didn't know, she didn't seek to light up the room because, to her, that didn't feel safe.

Conversely, if she went to a small dinner party with close friends (and even the previously-unknown friends of those friends), she could freely and easily open up and become the life of the party. Why? Because she felt safe there. And to her, safety was a major priority. Thus, creating safe situations for others was also important to her. It—safety—was a personal value that she wanted to extol in everything she did.

And remember, that is her value. It belongs entirely to her. You don't have to subscribe to it and she, thankfully, doesn't give a rip whether you have the same value or not. But as she carries out her life (especially after we broke this all down), a major priority to her is living in situations where she feels safe. It is one of her truly personal, personal values.

So, what traits help you define your value system? You know what, stop thinking about values at all for a moment. What traits define you? Are you outgoing? Funny? Shy? Opinionated? Thoughtful? Well-read?

Whatever it is, I want you to take the next 30 minutes and think about what you value about those traits of yours. For example, if you're well-read, does that come from a value of curiosity? Or maybe a value for the exchange of ideas? What's really behind these traits of yours? Stop everything you're doing and break your traits down as far as you possibly can. Then, once you've done that, try to recognize what personal values bubble to the surface.

Exercise #3: Explore whether there are values behind your values

Remember a few pages ago when, by describing an instance where she put her value system into action, Joan was able to list "compassion" as one of her truly personal, personal values? You didn't think I was just going to accept that without a challenge did you? If so, I'm truly disappointed that you haven't been paying attention to the words in this book.

After the brief exchange I shared earlier, Joan was quite happy to declare that compassion was a core value for her—especially compassion for people in need.

"So," I said with all the confidence of a person who is about to set her friend up for a fall, "do you always practice compassion for those in need?"

"I honestly can't say that I do," Joan replied. "That's why I struggle with listing compassion as a core value of mine." I asked her to expand on that.

"Let's say I'm driving in my car and someone ahead of me sits through a green light or they are driving under the speed limit. Intellectually, I realize that they may have something going on that's distracting them but in that moment, I am furious. That's not compassionate at all."

"So maybe you have a value that's deeper than compassion," I replied. "Let's explore that."

After some talking, Joan realized that one thing she values very highly is efficiency. Perhaps predictably, she then confessed that efficiency seemed, to her, to be a rather shallow value. We dug even deeper. Ultimately, what we settled on is that Joan has a very deep connection with the value of time. To her (and to me) time is too valuable a resource to simply be wasted.

Ever the proud author, I told Joan about the work we did in Chapter 1 about being intentional with your time. Finally, she connected very deeply with what turns out to be her most personal, personal value—using time in a meaningful way. You see, Joan has experienced the untimely deaths of a few key people in her life. From that, she grew to value time above almost anything else—because those close to her had lost it.

It's not to say that compassion isn't a value in Joan's life—it is. But by tracing her own lack of compassion back to its core, we were able to identify an even deeper value. One that Joan recognized she practices without compromise.

I encourage you to do the same if you, like Joan, are feeling like some of your core values aren't "core" enough. I also encourage you, like I did with her, to give yourself a break. Even if you aren't currently practicing your core values in every second of every day, there's hope. Indeed, that's what Being Bold is all about. Read on . . .

Exercise #4: BE BOLD

Finally, we've reached the main point of this Chapter! It isn't titled "Be Bold" just for the heck of it. The first part was defining those core personal values of yours. The harder part, as you've probably surmised by now, is choosing to Be Bold with them.

And, I'm not trying to be a jerk here but I'm guessing most of you are not Being Bold with your personal values. Why? Because society, our parents, our culture, our media—all of them are constantly telling us we need to put their values first. You can't Be Bold while you're devaluing your own values. So, shut all of those influences out immediately (actually, I told you to do that back when you were simply defining your truly personal, personal values—if you didn't do it then, for Pete's sake, do it NOW).

For purposes of this exercise, I want you to pick your top personal value. Got it in mind? Great! My question to you is this: what are you going to do in the next week to exemplify that value?

Let's go back to Joan since you now know her top value in such excruciating detail. As she and I were getting to the notion that not wasting time is a core value of hers, she expressed frustration with the inefficient traffic flow in her city. In her estimation, the traffic lights are antiquated and she spends half of her driving time sitting at red lights when there's no cross traffic. The situation frustrates the hell out of her because she is forced to spend so much time living the opposite of her core value. Or is she?

If Joan were to truly Be Bold with her value of time, wouldn't she look for a city commission she could sit on to help improve traffic flow throughout her region? Couldn't she run for city council? I mean, if that's a situation that is truly forcing her to compromise her core value, why not do something about it?

The examples are endless. Let's say the top value you picked for this exercise is creativity (one of my top five, by the way). Despite all the hard work it took for you to identify that truly personal, personal value in the first place, you've also recognized that you're not doing anything about it. In fact, you may be tempted to give me the same litany of excuses you used in Chapter 1 when we talked about being intentional with time . . . you've got kids to feed, a career to pursue, a house to clean, yada yada yada. I get it.

If you were earnestly going to Be Bold with your value of creativity, however, you would start making time for it TODAY. Maybe you keep a sketch pad by your bed and simply doodle for five minutes before you go to sleep. You could do that, right? Or maybe you commit to visiting a local art museum once a week to fuel your creative juices. The only thing standing between you and that simple goal is you, my friend.

Over time, you will see that when you're Being Bold with your personal values, you're living a happier life. You may be shocked, in fact, when the time you thought you didn't have for your own values suddenly appears in your schedule. You know what happens then? You're even happier and more fulfilled. This isn't rocket science, folks. It's about commitment to you.

And remember, Being Bold with your personal values is absolutely critical if you've recently gone through a life change that has thrown you off center. The best way to get back to YOU is identify your personal values, live them, and Be Bold with them. Be like Stacy. Find a way to make your personal values work with whatever your life looks like now.

In reality, all I'm asking you to do here is just an extension of what I asked you to do in Chapter 1. Again, that Chapter was focused on being intentional about your time. Don't you think it will be easier to do that now that you're allowing your very own, truly personal, personal values to guide you in that endeavor?

Remember a few paragraphs back when I asked you to identify your top personal value? What I want you to do right NOW is write down three different ways that you can live out that value within the next week. Feels good, right? But wait, there's more!

Now take the remaining personal values that you've identified and do the same thing. Write down three different ways that you will exemplify those values this week. Remember, I'm not asking you to spend 24/7 on these things. I'm asking you to make a digestible list that you can use to ignite your life of Being Bold.

After the first week is over, I'm guessing you'll be addicted to the process. Great! Repeat that same process every week for a year. Please hold your complaints. I know this will be hard for some of you. That's precisely why I don't ask you to make a list of 50 or more of your truly personal, personal values. Life would be impossible if we had to live all of those virtues boldly day in and day out.

If you're still not convinced, stop and visualize what your life will look like if you commit to this practice as I've asked. Eventually, you will stop living a life based on shoulds or should nots that come from other people. In fact, please stop 'shoulding' all over yourself, it is not becoming!

Do you know what else is going to happen? Well, for one thing, your Mission Essential will become more "essential." Your time will become more intentional. And now, because you have a defined list of values to guide you through every decision, you will only continue to get stronger, more powerful, happier, and truer to yourself. All the while, you will subtly realize that you no longer need to ask anyone else for permission. This is your life, guided by your values. Go forth and rock your life!

"You don't make mistakes.
Mistakes make you.
They make you smarter.
They make you stronger.
And more self-reliant. Fall on your face.
Fail spectacularly. Because when you fail,
you learn. When you fail, you live."

—Claudia Aronowitz

"How do you eat an elephant?
One bite at a time."

—Creighton Abrams, Jr.

Eleven

Fail Spectacularly

I am giving you two quotes for the price of one. I know you can handle it. You are welcome.

As you can tell from the opening quotes, I'm not the first person to discuss these topics. I do, however, approach them differently. For example, when it comes to the idea of "failing spectacularly," I want to rob those two words of their separateness.

To me, "FailingSpectacularly" is the proper spelling—otherwise, there's too much emphasis on failing. I also don't like the idea of FailingSpectacularly as a singular life mantra. Rather, it is the fork one should use to eat that elephant, one bite at a time.

I know, I know . . . we've got a lot of unpacking to do here . Let's get started.

In Chapter 9, we discussed how you can find your Mission Essential. Have you done it? If not, go back and do the exercises. You'll need your ME to grasp how FailingSpectacularly at eating the elephant can help you enact (or supercharge) that power.

Also, in Chapter 10, we tackled the concept of **Being Bold**. Again, if you haven't absorbed that material, you need to go back and do it now. Why are you taking shortcuts? If I wanted you to skip ahead to this chapter, I would have left the others out or put this one first. Pay attention!

Ok, good. You're back. You have a defined Mission Essential and you're ready to Be Bold.

Finally, we can take a look at FailingSpectacularly at eating the elephant. Before we do that, however, let's break down the two concepts that permeate this Chapter.

FailingSpectacularly

FailingSpectacularly, at its core, is nothing more than a commitment to trying the things you've always wanted to do but never **allowed** yourself to get around to.

When you set out to FailSpectacularly, you actually let go of your expectations about the outcome. You begin the journey with the story that the outcome does not matter one bit. Once you have that mindset, the fear of failure necessarily must (and will) evaporate.

FailingSpectacularly reinforces the idea of "being" and not necessarily "doing." "Being" a person who tries new things, "being" a person who is willing to be vulnerable, "being" a person who is confident enough in who they are to push their growth edge. It allows a person to take chances and not be defined by a specific outcome that defines how "good" or "successful" a person is by what they have achieved. FailingSpectacularly puts an increased value on the **journey**.

So, stop for a minute and think. What are some of the things you've always wanted to do but have been too afraid to try? What internal stories do you tell yourself for why you can't do them? Who in your life has conditioned you to believe you cannot achieve these things (including yourself)?

Now that you've had a moment to think, I'm going to give you some critical advice—Get over it! Instead of holding back, we're going to get you to the place where you are dedicated to FailingSpectacularly at those precise things.

Before you start making excuses about your fear of failure, hear me out. FailingSpectacularly is not about failing. In fact, it is nothing short of winning. This is because when you FailSpectacularly, there are only two possible outcomes:

1. You succeed; or

2. You learn.

Remember the Warner Brothers cartoon, Road Runner? That show used to frustrate the hell out of me. Coyote would enact this great plan for catching the Road Runner, and invariably something would happen, and the Road Runner would get away scot free.

Mmmeeep meep!

Damn you Coyote! You know that ridge is not stable enough to hold your contraption. You know the Road Runner will always run in the opposite direction of where you set your trap. Yet you give up too soon. You learned a couple things, use those things you learned and go back and try your plan again. And keep trying until you are enjoying a muscly, sinewy leg tonight for dinner.

Coyote always gave up. Hence he lived his life as a hopeless loser.

Think about that for a moment. You're going to start trying the things that scare you the most. You're either going to be great at them or you're going to learn from your mistakes. In the latter scenario, you're now in the perfect position to try again, absent those mistakes. What you're not going to do is be like Coyote—a guy who kept trying but never learned from past let downs. This is the critical difference between simply failing and FailingSpectacularly.

Once you commit to FailingSpectacularly, you can try again and again and again until all the mistakes are gone, and you find success. And now you've achieved what no one (cough, cough . . . you) thought you could.

Good job, you!

Since I just used the "S" word, we should probably take a quick diversion to talk about the concept of success.

What is success?

Lots of people have lots of ideas about what success is. Culture, social media, our families, our friends—all of these influencers are constantly giving us their ideas of what success looks like. If you open the typical women's magazine, success may look like flawlessly contoured makeup, the perfect wardrobe, an attractive, wealthy partner, and a meticulously manicured home in precisely the right neighborhood. Our culture may tell us that success comes from marriage and children. Our family may have conditioned us to believe that success comes only from financial stability.

I have to tell you that I don't give a rip about any of that. It's not that I don't strive for some of those things in my personal life (who doesn't want to highlight their fabulous cheekbones?). It's just that I care more about my own (and your own) personal ideas about success. In every moment of every day, I want you to think about what success looks like to you.

That's where the elephant concept comes in.

FailingSpectacularly isn't a one-time deal that changes your entire life for the better (although, by the time you've eaten the whole elephant, that may be the result!).

FailingSpectacularly is a tool you can use to get yourself to take each bite. In short, FailingSpectacularly is about doing the things you want to do (or not do) today, right now, in this very moment that will help you reach your wildest dreams.

Here's an example to illustrate just how small each bite can be.

The elusive souffle

Martha grew up without a mother. Her father worked two jobs and never really had time to cook for her, let alone teach her how to cook. Nonetheless, as Martha grew into adulthood, she learned to love farm-to-table restaurants, cooking magazines, and all the cooking shows she could find on TV. Once she got her own apartment, she tried cooking from time to time. Mostly simple stuff—baked chicken, casseroles, and spaghetti with homemade sauce. Secretly, she longed to become a chef.

To Martha, the ultimate cooking challenge was a souffle. She had seen all the greats prepare this exquisite dish on TV—the Barefoot Contessa, Giada De Laurentiis, and even some of the contestants on the Iron Chef. Martha knew that cooking the perfect souffle was the pinnacle of cooking. If she could master that one thing, maybe she could make her way to culinary school and eventually become a chef. All of that seemed far-fetched, however. Thus, she avoided the one thing that, in her own mind, stood between her and her ultimate dream.

Do you see how she attached so much meaning in her mind to "doing" that exceedingly difficult souffle, that it felt like too big of a goal to ever succeed? And in turn, the goal seemed so big that the thought of failure was crippling?

Don't be the Coyote!

Martha repeated this failure-fairytale until she got sick of hearing herself make excuses. One day, she simply decided that when it came to the elusive souffle, she was going to FailSpectacularly. It was just one recipe. If she screwed it up, no one would know but her. She pulled her favorite cookbook off the shelf, put on her apron, and gave it a whirl. And you know what? She got exactly what she expected. Her methods didn't work. The souffle failed to rise.

The next day, she made another one. After doing some research, she figured the base was too thick in the original recipe. That condition didn't allow the egg whites to rise. She remedied that problem the second time around. No luck. The souffle still didn't rise.

On the third day, after still more research, she whipped her egg whites right before adding them to the dish. She did this because she had read that "tired" egg whites could cause the souffle not to rise. And on this third attempt—success!

I can hear many of you grumbling . . . "Who cares? It's just a stupid souffle! Her success isn't going to change the world." And *that* is exactly where you're wrong.

She tried and she failed. Then she failed again. She learned. Then she succeeded. If you don't see the beauty in that, you're reading the wrong book.

By FailingSpectacularly at making a souffle, Martha ate the first bite of her elephant (becoming a chef). In essence, the perfect souffle was the gatekeeper to her doing other things in life she desperately wanted to do. After the souffle, she was ready to take another bite of elephant meat. But we'll return to Martha's story later. For now, let's move on to the concept of eating that elephant.

How do you eat an elephant?

We all know the answer to this old riddle. Of course, you eat an elephant one bite at a time. Duh! But is that really the full answer or is there more to it? I'm suggesting there's a lot more to it and I'm going to give you a gross analogy to help you understand.

Let's say you actually do have an elephant that you need to eat.

I don't know where you got it; hopefully it's not an endangered species. The point is, you have an elephant carcass laying in your backyard and you have to eat the darn thing.

You could certainly go into the back yard and try to eat it with a knife and fork—one bite at a time. If you do that, chances are you'll end up with a yard full of flies, maggots, and rotting elephant flesh before you can ever choke the whole thing down.

Instead, you'd be wise to say to yourself, "Ok, I have this dead elephant. I know I need to eat the whole thing and that I have to do it one bite at a time. But I'll never get it done before the meat spoils. What I need is a plan for eating this elephant!" That, my friends, is the point. You have to have a plan for eating your elephant before it spoils.

Let's go back to Martha because the whole dead-elephant thing is so disgusting. Martha's ultimate dream (her elephant) was to become a chef. The first bite of the elephant was making a souffle. She succeeded at that, and that's great, but now she has to make a plan for eating the rest.

For Martha, that involved many steps. She knew she needed to go to culinary school. But she had a full-time job and no savings to speak of to use for tuition money. Plus, she needed a lot more practice and experience before she could apply to culinary school. For the past ten years, she had been an accountant. She'd never even worked in a restaurant. She had a mortgage to pay, a steep car payment, and around $10,000 in credit card debt.

When you look at Martha's "elephant" through that lens, it seems impossible to eat. You may be telling yourself there is no way she can take all those bites before the thing rots in her yard (just to spell out the analogy for those of you who are multitasking—there's no way she can take all the steps she needs to take before her dream of becoming a chef dies). Oh, ye of little faith! Read on.

What I suggested to Martha when she called me is that she make a plan for exactly how she could eat that elephant. I told her that, in reality, she was going to have to put a lot of meat in the freezer. Nonetheless, if she had a solid plan, she would eventually eat the whole damn thing. Here's a portion of the plan we came up with:

Martha would sell her home to pay off her credit card debt and the remaining balance on her car loan.

She would put the rest of the money in a short-term investment account with minimal risk.

Next, she would rent a small house or apartment where she could live comfortably, but for hundreds of dollars less per month than she was paying on her mortgage.

She would quit her job as an accountant and seek a job working in a restaurant or commercial kitchen.

She would reach out to her favorite local chefs and ask them to serve as a mentor.

She would apply to culinary school.

She would speak to the student loan department at her school about financing options.

She would attend culinary school and graduate in the top 5% of her class.

She would seek out sous chef positions at her favorite restaurants.

Eventually, she would become the head chef she always dreamed of.

I want you to notice a couple things about Martha's plan. First, she was never going to eat her entire elephant in one day. In fact, most of those bites included several "mini-bites" that Martha had to take before she could move on. (You don't have all week to read about Martha, so I've given you a summary).

Second, just about every step along the way was terrifying for her. But what do we do when faced with the terrifying things that lead us to our dreams? If you can't answer that question, go back and read this chapter again. If you were paying attention, you know the answer is a resounding "FailSpectacularly."

Yay! You have so got this!

Seemingly insurmountable hurdles

I want to take a moment to address what several of you nay-sayers are thinking—"I can't possibly eat the elephant. My bites are too big! I have children! I have a husband! I have to work three jobs just to pay the rent . . . I don't have time for anything else!"

Calm down. I hear you. All of those things may seem insurmountable today. But unless you're living in solitary confinement with no hope of ever being released from prison, there are little, tiny, baby bites that you can start to take in order to FailSpectacularly at eating your elephant.

For example, I get it that your children have to be your first priority. Mine are for me, too. I was a single mom of two girls when I started eating my elephant (stay tuned for the stunning details in the next section). I worked full time, I had a business to run, kids to shuttle to their events, meals to cook, blah, blah, blah, etc.

What I'm telling you is that once you decide to eat an elephant, you also get to decide how big the bites are going to be. When I started my project, I had to carve out time that was just for me. At first, that meant staying up an hour later than normal so I could work on MY stuff.

Later, it involved getting my girls involved in their own elephant eating a couple times a month. Whatever you need to achieve, the answers are there. You just need to plan carefully and execute fearlessly. Keep reading.

Putting it all together

In order to FailSpectacularly at eating the elephant, all you have to do is ask yourself two questions: (1) what dream have I been too scared to pursue?; and (2) can that dream be achieved if I break the process up into digestible chunks?

For me, it was a sculpture project. I grew up in a family of artists and, consequently, there was always an unsaid expectation to become a great artist, or at least some form of an artist. I was born with Bohemian blood in me and we all know how creative those gypsies are!

Notwithstanding my lineage, I was scared to even begin a project that I had been thinking about for decades. What if I failed? What if the sculpture was terrible and I let everyone around me down? What if no one wanted to look at it except for me? What if people laughed at it?

Then, one day, I decided I was going to FailSpectacularly and I began eating my elephant—the one project that had been rattling around in my brain for all those years. So what if it wasn't perfect? So what if no one else liked it? I simply knew in that moment that the time had come to begin the project. I knew I did not want to be on my deathbed and wonder "what if . . . ?" I got to work making a plan for how I was going to eat my elephant and then I gave myself permission to FailSpectacularly at every bite.

This was no small project. It involved the age-old question that people invariably ask on first dates or at cocktail parties: "If you could invite anyone, dead or alive to dinner, who would it be?" Now, for most people, the answer consists of a series of political figures, authors, or celebrities. For me, I was interested in creating brand new characters to invite to my dinner party.

And that was the project—I wanted to create the busts of 12 unknown, fictional people that I thought would be interesting to sit down and talk to over the dinner table. I believe that we all have a story, we all have something fascinating in us, and I wanted to pull that out of the most seemingly normal people.

Before I could get started on such an ambitious project, I first had to connect with my intrinsic purpose; or, what we talked about in Chapter 9 as our individual Mission Essential. Because my ME is "Go Big or Go Home," I first had to promise myself that if I was going to start this, I was going to see it through to the end. That involved a lot more than driving down to the art store and purchasing the easiest materials for a beginner to use.

Nope. I scoffed at the idea of molding my sculptures out of something normal like clay. Instead, I decided to create the busts of my "guests" out of concrete. That was the first bite of my elephant. I had never sculpted with concrete. Therefore, I started reading everything I could about the medium. I bought some concrete to work with and gave myself permission to FailSpectacularly as I built the early prototypes.

And what a mess I made! A glorious, oozing concrete mess about which I could proudly say—nope that is not it.

Along the way, I learned many lessons about things like concrete-to-water ratios, the crumbly nature of concrete, how to build the base structures that would hold each bust, and so on. Once I had done all that, I knew the process of eating the elephant had begun.

Go-Big-or-Go-Home-Christina was going to eat the whole damn thing.

Consequently, I now had to *plan* for how I was going to eat the rest of this gigantic creature. For me, that meant creating project folders and files that would contain my research, notes, sketches, and other ideas relating to the project. The whole plan took up an entire drawer in my file cabinet. And, although that was intimidating, I was already giving myself permission to do two critical things: (1) only eat one bite at a time; and (2) FailSpectacularly at every step along the way.

I won't bore you with every excruciating detail. Suffice it to say that five years after deciding to eat this elephant, the sculptures were completed. That doesn't mean the project was done, however. No, I still had a few more bites to pull out of the freezer. For example, I worked with a local writer to come up with biographies for each of my guests. I created a website to showcase my work. I entered the pieces into art shows all over the world. I was featured by a gallery in Palm Springs, California, and was accepted into several art exhibitions.

By FailingSpectacularly every step of the way, I learned a ton. That may be the understatement of the year.

After all of that, I can tell you that my elephant tasted great. And I'm ready for another. What the hell do you think this book is about? (It is my current elephant.)

The same thing can happen for you. What scares you? When are you going to start making a plan for doing it? Why not today? This is the part of the chapter when I ask you to put down the book and meditate for a while. What in your life have you never done because your internal narrative told you couldn't or (God forbid) shouldn't?

Pick the book back up when you have a list of three to four things, you're ready to FailSpectacularly at. Then pick one, and we'll start making a plan for how you're going to eat that elephant.

An exercise in elephant eating

Welcome back! I have to say that one of the things I love the most about FailingSpectacularly at eating the elephant is that it is directly in line with the title of this book (*You Don't Need Permission*, for those of you with short memories).

Once you decide to FailSpectacularly at eating the elephant, you're essentially saying to yourself, "hey, me ... go ahead and do that thing. I give me permission to try. I absolutely cannot fail so long as I learn something along the way." Also, when you combine FailingSpectacularly with elephant eating, you make seemingly monumental tasks into reasonable challenges.

Ready to get started? Too bad. Let's do it anyway. Here are the step-by-step questions you need to be asking yourself in order to make this happen:

How to eat your elephant

1. What elephant did you decide to eat at the end of the last section?

2. How will your particular Mission Essential (ME) assist you in eating that elephant? (If you don't have an answer to this question, you need more work on your ME. Go back to Chapter 9).

3. Are you ready to Be Bold? (If your answer is "no," you need to spend more time with Chapter 10 before you eat this elephant).

4. Why haven't you eaten this particular elephant before? (*i.e.*, what stories have you been telling yourself to explain why you can't get this done?)

5. What are the 10 biggest hurdles between your life today and eating the whole elephant?

6. For each of the 10 things listed in response to the last question, list three actions you can take to overcome each

hurdle (for example, if one of your hurdles was "I don't have the money to get started," list three things you might be able to do to bring in extra income).

7. Now, go through each of the 30 action items you've just listed, and ask yourself "am I ready to FailSpectacularly at this?" Remember, FailingSpectacularly means giving yourself permission to try, regardless of the outcome. FailingSpectacularly means being committed to learning from your mistakes along the way. FailingSpectacularly sometimes means picking yourself up, dusting yourself off, and trying again.

8. Can you do that? For all 30 action items?

9. If you have identified action items you're not ready to FailSpectacularly at, try breaking them down into smaller bites. For example, if your action item was "Get out from under the burden of my mortgage," but you're not willing to sell your house right now, try to think about smaller bites you might take. Can you rent out a room in your house? Can you refinance at a better rate? Sometimes, you just need to refocus on smaller solutions.

10. Remind yourself of your Mission Essential. I can tell this exercise is making you weary.

11. Once you've broken down your plan for eating the elephant into completely digestible bites, it's time to start FailingSpectacularly.

Have fun and remember as long as you're learning, you're **not** failing.

"Look well into thyself; there is a source of strength which will always spring up if thou wilt always look."

—Marcus Aurelius

Twelve

Innate Supreme Wisdom

*Author s Note: *Writing this book has been an amazing journey. When I first began, I had an outline of the chapters I wanted to present and a rough idea of the order in which they should appear in the book. Very quickly, however, I learned that I had no interest in writing the book in that order. Rather, I skipped from early chapters to late chapters to middle chapters whenever I felt like it, cuz that's the kind of girl I am. I don't need permission to write my book any damn way I want.*

I began writing this chapter—which is largely focused on positive tools for relaxation, positivity, and strength—three weeks ago. At the time, there was a new illness hitting the news called the "Coronavirus" (or COVID-19). I didn't think much about it. Over the last few weeks, however, the virus has become a global pandemic. In the U.S., entire cities are shut down and people are being asked to isolate from others. And I'm realizing, in this moment, that this chapter is especially important to the world (and to me) right now.

Ultimately, I just wanted to share with you all from the outset how grateful I am for this journey and how fortunate I feel to be able to focus on positivity in a world that presently looks rather bleak. Now, back to the chapter I intended to write . . .

No matter who you are, what you do, and how content you are with your life on a daily basis, we all experience hardships. Big hardships and little hardships. Life is hard, and I subscribe to the idea that it is supposed to be. The challenge of living a fulfilled, happy, balanced life is not for the faint of heart. It is through the tough times that we grow, learn about ourselves, and pay those gifts forward.

When tough times do arise, there is a real temptation to lean on other people. And, of course, that's ok. It is wonderful to have a shoulder to cry on and a trusted other to whom we turn when life throws us curveballs. Our friends and family can provide tremendous support and love when we need it most.

You must trust me, however, when I tell you that those wonderful, supportive people are never enough to see you through the rough times. You must—absolutely MUST—be able to rely on yourself more than anyone else. Whether your troubles are massive (grief or pandemic) or relatively trivial (just a run-of-the-mill bad day), you are going to need tools that you can deploy to live through the stress.

The good news is, those tools are plentiful. They are available to you right now, in this very moment. And, best of all, the vast majority of them are free and accessible 24 hours a day, seven days a week. In fact, most of these tools involve an innate supreme wisdom that lives inside of you already. All you have to do is tap into them and commit to making them a part of your journey. The tough times are coming (indeed, as I write this, they are here). It is nice to be prepared and have a few tools to lean on, to support ourselves, and help us reconnect to our source.

I have to tell you—I am thrilled to introduce you to (or remind you of) some of my favorite tools. These are the powerful, life-changing practices that I have used—and will continue to use—any time I feel the need for balance in my life (that is code for every day . . .). If these tools help you when times are tough, doesn't it make sense to continue practicing them when things are going well? If you do, you will only be that much stronger when events take a turn again.

Mind, Body, and Soul

As I began work on this chapter, I realized that many of the tools I planned to write about could be said to enhance one's mind, body, AND soul. That said, for you, some tools may fit in one category more so than another. For example, while I may see outdoor exercise as something that nurtures my body, you may see it as something that nurtures your soul. That's ok. Neither of us are wrong. Keep that in mind as we move forward.

By now, you know me pretty well. Therefore, you won't be shocked when I tell you how I'm going to start this chapter—by presenting you with another challenge. First, I want you to read through my summary of all these amazing tools. Then, I want you to pick one from each category that you can commit to practicing for two months. (Of course, if you start something and it doesn't resonate with you, don't make it into a chore—try something else from that category.) My point is, just try to give yourself a little boost in each area and give yourself the time for each practice to really make an impact on your life.

Here's the part I wanted you to keep in mind. If, as you read through the tools, you don't agree with my categorization of a certain tool as principally enhancing the mind, body, or soul—don't worry about it. Regardless of my subjective grouping of these tools, I want you to practice:

One tool that YOU believe will enhance your mind;

One tool that YOU believe will enhance your body; and

One tool that YOU believe will enhance your soul.

Got it? Good. The key is for you to simply seek improvement in those three areas in the way that seems best for you.

After two to three months, I can almost guarantee that you'll be feeling more fierce. More calm. More focused. More grounded. Stronger. Smarter. More lovable. More loving. And let's be honest, we could all benefit from that.

Let's get started . . .

Tools for your mind

Visualization

If you haven't heard of visualization as a tool for success, it is possible that you've been living under a rock without WiFi. You may have heard of "The Secret," vision boards, the Law of Attraction, or any of the million other labels that people use to describe this wonderful tool.

Regardless of the label, the practice is essentially the same—and it is as simple as it is powerful.

All you need to do is set aside some time—preferably at least 10 minutes a day—to focus on and picture (i.e., visualize) your ideal life. That's it. Pretty simple, right? It really is that easy but there are intricacies to the practice. Everybody does it differently, yet there are some common themes that permeate each method.

In just about every case, for example, it is important that you are: (1) alone; (2) in a quiet space; (3) sober; (4) able to really concentrate, uninterrupted, for 10 minutes or more; and (5) able to repeat this practice regularly over the course of your lifetime. Let's assume for a minute that you have all that under control. Now what?

Some people choose to see their life as a movie. They shut their eyes and let their life story play out in their mind. Other people cut out pictures from magazines that exemplify their dreams. Still others write journal entries about the way their life is going to play out in the future. The key, regardless of your method, is to always focus on your *ideal* life. Don't be afraid to rely on your emotions. Allow your five senses to form a complete picture, to make it come alive. If you sit down for a visualization session and find that all you can do is focus on the problems of the day, or worry about problems that might arise at some later date, you need to stop and try again when your mind is clear.

The reason for this is best summed up in the age-old principle that "thoughts are things." In fact, research and meditation practice have proven this theory through the ages. If you want to look at the practice from a negative standpoint, consider this quote often attributed to Lara Casey: "Worrying is like praying for what you don't want." Visualization, on the other hand, is like praying for what you *do* want. And, honestly, consider how central prayer has been to nearly every culture in every century. Prayer is a form of visualization. Or, perhaps more concisely stated, visualization is much like prayer, but without the religious connotations attached.

And, what is prayer if not a sincere concentration on the things you desire in life? With prayer, however, we're often asking a higher power to bless us with something. With visualization, we are keenly focused on the idea that we can—and will—achieve desired results for ourselves. We can see it, hear it, taste it, smell it, and touch it. Most importantly, as we visualize it, we believe it. We feel it in our bones.

I don't want you to be fooled. I know I referred to this practice as simple—and it is in principle. In reality, it can be *hard* to remain confident in your visualization and your belief that you can achieve some enormous goal. Sometimes, old doubts will sneak in. In other circumstances, you may hear a loved one's voice saying, "you'll never be able to [fill in the blank]." The first key to successful visualization is to block out all of that negative messaging, regardless of its source. For visualization to work, you have to let go of earthly trappings and just *feel*.

The second key is to *practice*. Look, you're probably not going to sit down on a Monday, visualize a million dollars in your bank account, and have it appear on Tuesday. If, on the other hand, you spend 10 minutes every morning for a year visualizing yourself with financial freedom, chances are that vision will come to fruition in one way or another. Consistency is critical. And, best of all, it is completely up to you.

Mindfulness

Chances are, you've heard of mindfulness, even if you've never tried it. That's not surprising given that, according to some sources, it is a practice that originated within the Hindu religion as far back as 1,500 BC. If you think about it in that light, something that has been around for over 3,500 years can't be all bad, can it?

At its core, mindfulness is a form of meditation where practitioners become supremely focused on their existence in the present moment. During a mindfulness session, one focuses on their own body, their breathing, the way their skin and muscles feel, and even the temperature in the room. One of the great benefits of mindfulness is that, when practiced correctly, it can draw your attention completely away from the problems, worries, and distractions that are otherwise infecting your life. And, by focusing heavily on slow, deep, consistent breathing, a person can actually reduce their stress level in a relatively short period of time.

Sounds easy, right? Well, not so fast, Buddy!

Mindfulness is actually a fairly difficult state to achieve. People throughout the ages have struggled with the "monkey mind." If you don't know what I mean, sit quietly for a minute and just watch how your brain swings from one idea to another with no apparent rhyme or reason. This is especially true in this day in age, when we are used to literally dozens of messages flying through our minds at any given moment. Whether it is stress about bills, the "ding" on our phones when a new message is received, or the distant sound of a police siren, our minds are constantly bombarded with the distractions of everyday life.

With mindfulness, the goal is to set all of that aside and just be in your own body for a period of time. This practice will teach you to be in control of your mind, while still showing yourself compassion. It will give you the self-discipline to be able to sit down and focus on an idea or task for the amount of time needed to really consider it.

There is a supreme mindset called "flow" that is the ultimate form of mindfulness. Maybe you have felt it when you were so engrossed with a project that nothing else entered your mind. Do you remember how exquisite that felt? If you become serious about your mindfulness practice, you will feel this supreme state more often. This also means you'll be able to get that monkey back under control!

While I have found great peace in my life through practicing mindfulness, I'm not here to teach you how to do it. My job is to introduce you to the possibility—your job is to find a way to achieve it. The good news is, there are plenty of resources to get you started (many of them free). For example, you might start with a website that gives in-depth instruction on how to work towards mindfulness.

If, like me, this practice resonates with you, you might want to go further with your practice. As I sit here writing this book, I'm very much looking forward to a mindfulness retreat that I plan to attend in a few months. I'll tell you all about it in the next book.

Journaling

Have you ever, even once in your life, been able to read something that you wrote long ago? It could have been a classroom assignment, a pre-teen diary, or a short story. Regardless, every single thing that you write is terribly enlightening when you go back and read it years later.

Of course, this is particularly true with private journals. There's something incredibly freeing about confiding in ourselves. When we do that, we have the opportunity to be authentic in a way that we could never be with others. We can reveal our greatest joys, biggest failures, most terrifying fears, and most embarrassing moments. And, with a little luck, the only audience is ourselves.

I want you to stop and really think about that for a moment. Keeping a journal is like having a friend that you NEVER have to tell a fib to. As an added bonus, that friend never, ever, forgets anything we tell her and never spills our secrets to anyone else. That friend lets us revisit her whenever we want. When we do go back to her, she may enlighten us. She may scare us. She may make us feel triumphant with progress or mortified by how stuck we are. In any event, she helps us grow.

As an added bonus, journaling feels really great in the moment. There's something about vomiting all of our thoughts out on paper that somehow absolves us from the heaviness of the day. In other words, journaling can be incredibly powerful for your present and for your future. You can do it any time of day and in any format you choose. So . . . why not give this one a try?

Tools for your soul

Gratitude

I actually struggled with whether this practice should be considered a Mind Tool or a Soul Tool. In recent years, there has been a lot of scientific research on the positive effects that gratitude can have on our brains. That research almost demands that this be considered a Mind Tool. My own personal journey with gratitude was so powerful to my soul, however, that I've decided to place this tool here. Honestly,

I actually don't care how we classify it. I think this tool is so powerful (and so easy) that everyone should use it every single day of their lives.

As for me, I found this practice at a particularly low point in my life. A cherished relationship had ended suddenly with all sorts of unexpected deceit and infidelity. I was at my wits end for months, wondering what I could have done differently to avoid that painful and humiliating result. I beat myself up emotionally on a daily basis. After all, if it wasn't my fault, whose was it? I was merciless in my judgment of myself.

And then, one morning, I was just so sick of feeling sad. I decided I needed to do something—anything—to pull myself out of it. Quite serendipitously and without any research, I decided to start keeping track of the things I was grateful for.

I remember that morning very well. I was sitting at the kitchen table, having my morning coffee, and dreading another day filled with depression and doubt. There was a spiral-bound notebook sitting on the table that I used for work, though my ability to work had been severely reduced due to my depression. Almost out of the blue, I picked up the notebook and a nearby pen and wrote down three things I was grateful for: (1) my dogs, who were always happy to be with me despite my despair; (2) the cool little cabin on the water I was staying in at the time; and (3) a couple of dear friends who lived a few houses down.

That sounds easy, right? It wasn't. I was so low that being grateful for anything was hard. Nonetheless, for the next several months, I committed to starting every day by writing down at least three things I was grateful for. And you know what happened? Each day, almost without trying, the list got longer. Soon, I was writing down five things. Then 10. Within a month I was filling pages of the things I had to be grateful for.

Without even realizing it at the time, the more I focused on gratitude, the less depressed I was. Science would tell us that gratitude was literally rewiring my brain. It's a process called "neuroplasticity." That basically means that you can retrain your brain's neural pathways to do different things—in this case, from being focused on depression to being focused on gratitude (which feels a lot like happiness). If you've never had your life centered around gratitude, I can tell you that it is a phenomenal feeling. And, compared to depression, well, it's a complete game changer.

I should include a word of caution here. If you lean toward depression generally, you will need to continue to practice gratitude in order for it to dominate your brain. If you stop, those old neural pathways to sadness may creep back in. The good news is that gratitude is so easy. But, as with visualization, it needs to become a daily part of your life in order for it to remain effective.

Why don't we start right now? Write down three things you're grateful for. Even if you had a deliriously dreadful day, it can't hurt to try, can it? And if you like what you've done, write down three more tomorrow. And however many things pop into your brain the next day. Keep going. See if it doesn't change your life in ways you never expected.

Tapping

Tapping is premised on literally "tapping into" your body's 12 meridian points. I can hear your cynicism now: "what the hell is a meridian point?" Simply put, your meridian points are pathways for your body's energy channels. I still hear all the naysayers balking at this. If you don't buy into your body as a source of universal flow and energy, that's cool . . . just move on. If you are open to that concept, however, keep reading.

Modern tapping involves focusing on a negative force in your life (and the resolution to that situation) while physically tapping on your body's meridians. The theory is that the tapping, when combined with this sort of focus, will return the body and mind to a state of balance.

There are a ton of resources available online to help you in this endeavor. Tapping can be a consistent strategy that you use on your own to restore balance and calm to your life in so many different areas—from relationships and trauma, to finance and physical health. In my experience, it is a very subtle but powerful release for energy that is blocked.

I was a stay at home mom for many, many years. When my ex-husband and I divorced, my resume was less than stellar. Shit, to be honest I couldn't even find it and even if I'd been able to, it needed to be updated drastically. Here was a likely conversation as I navigated my way back into the workforce. "Yes sir, I have stayed at home and taken care of my family for the last twelve years but I am sure I can now function in a professional office. Excuse me, you have a smudge of mustard on your face, here let me get that for you," as I lick a napkin that was scrunched up in my pocket.

I had not had the opportunity to show anyone where my value was in a working environment and so I sat down one day and reviewed my finances and, in particular, exactly what I needed to keep me and my girls afloat. I figured out my minimum and started tapping on the incredible fear behind making money and being able to pay for everything with so little to work with. I was scared but I was willing to try anything. I would tap every day, and I would start with the gnarliest, most negative fear I could muster. Some days, I would be in tears . . . but I kept tapping.

One day a new job opportunity just landed in my lap, purely out of coincidence . . . or was it? At the time, I had been working part-time for a non-profit and suddenly a five-business conglomerate asked me to come do the same work on a full-time basis. They even asked me to name my price. Hell yeah! I can do that. As I write this, I'm realizing that I have drifted away from my practice. This is a perfect reminder to take it up again. .

Creativity

I'm an artist, so I like to think everybody has a little bit of creativity in their souls. For me, starting up a new art project is like breathing in the elixir of life—it feels great no matter how shitty I may be feeling otherwise. Anyone who considers themselves an artist definitely knows this feeling and I don't need to spend pages reminding you how important it is that you foster your creative spirit.

The person I do need to reach is the woman who has long been telling herself "I can't." You know what I'm talking about. Closeted creative people have a billion reasons not to create. You don't think you're good enough. You've never been trained. You don't have time. There are other things that are more important.

Stop it! All I'm asking you to do is to spend 10 to 15 minutes a day being creative in a way that is meaningful for you. For a lot of people, that simply means buying (and using) an adult coloring book. For others, it means giving themselves permission to create art—any piece of art—even if they think it will be "bad." For still others, it can mean a much-needed trip to a museum to simply soak in the wonder of someone else's art.

You get my drift here, right? Creativity is a universe and you get to decide how that universe manifests for you. The important thing is that you give yourself permission to play, to create, to experiment. It is a freeing experience that will release you from all of the expectations and responsibilities of adulthood. You're welcome.

Volunteering

If you need to read a long-winded section on why volunteering will enhance your soul, then I'm guessing you've never volunteered. In my view, it almost doesn't matter what you volunteer to do, it is the simple act of helping someone else without expecting anything in return that feels so ridiculously good. And the great news is, no matter what you're passionate about in life, you can find volunteer opportunities that meet your interests.

Don't believe me? Try these on for size:

If your passion is . . .
Art . . . you make like volunteering for . . .
- The local art museum

- A childrens' art project

- An independent art show

If your passion is . . .
The environment . . . you make like volunteering for . . .
- A beach cleanup

- A trail-building project

- Organizing a carpool

If your passion is . . .
Family . . . you may like volunteering for . . .

- Big Brothers & Sisters of America

- A foster grandparent program

- Your church potluck

If your passion is . . .
Sports . . . you may like volunteering for . . .

- A youth sports league

- A route helper for a marathon

- A lifeguard

If your passion is . . .
Helping those in need . . . you may like volunteering for . . .

- A food bank

- A homeless shelter

- A family planning clinic

You get the picture, right? Wherever there are people, there are people who need help. And while they will undoubtedly benefit from your time, my guess is you will be the one who sees the greatest benefit.

Tools for your body

Yoga

Yoga is another one of those ancient practices that is so beneficial that it couldn't help but reappear in modern times and in every corner of the globe. In fact, today it may be more popular than ever. And it's no wonder.

For those of you who have not tried it, yoga is much more than a series of stretches (although that is an important part of the practice). Yoga has a lot to do with mindfulness (see above), control of your breathing, relaxation, and an overall sense of calm and wellness.

Importantly, there are almost as many different kinds of yoga as there are different kinds of people. With a little research and some "clinical trials," you just may find your jam. Whether it's Bikram Yoga (aka "hot" yoga), Yin Yoga (a series of slow, methodical stretches), or anything in between, chances are yoga will be transformative to your life.

While I'm no doctor, I'm certainly an observer of human behavior. And in observing other people get serious about yoga, I've seen them: (1) lose weight; (2) become better athletes; (3) increase calm in their lives; (4) increase focus and awareness; and (5) become incredibly toned and fit.

Individual exercise

Some people really don't like to exercise around other people. For them, it is the act of challenging themselves that matters. For example, have you ever known a runner? These folks can strap on a pair of shoes, put on some headphones, and run for hours. I don't get it but those who do tell me it is incredibly gratifying. They talk of the runner's high, the increased cardiovascular capacity, and the peace they get from it. Those are all amazing things!

And, of course, running is not the only form of individual exercise you can pursue. Some people like to shoot hoops by themselves. Others do online Zumba classes in the isolation of their own living rooms. Still others walk, swim, participate in archery, fish, or do any of a million other things that give them: (1) exercise; and (2) solitude. So, whatever your jam is, get to it.

It's important to note here that I want you to do all of this for your individual well-being. Even a few minutes of exercise a day for the two-to-three month period will make a difference. I'm not asking you to do this to lose weight (although you might). I'm not asking you to beat your personal best in anything (although you might). I'm simply asking you to do this enough that you feel better from it. For some of you, that will mean training for a marathon. Others will be satisfied with doing 20 pushups a day. Both are completely reasonable outcomes. As the folks at Nike say, the important thing is that you "Just Do It."

Of course, if you have neglected this for a while, get the thumbs up from your doctor so you are doing positive things for yourself and not tearing yourself down further.

Team sports

If you're the type of person who needs a little more socialization with your exercise, consider participating in team sports. Even if you've never played basketball, baseball, football, soccer, or any other team sport, I can almost guarantee there's a league out there for you somewhere.

In fact, when I moved to Portland, Oregon, a few years ago, I was anxious to meet new people and to get a little exercise. You know what I did? I joined an adult kickball team. And guess what? Before the first season was through, I had a gaggle of new friends, weekly events to look forward to, and the physical benefits of getting my butt out on the field and running around.

While kickball may not be your thing, I bet there's a league out there for you. How about bowling? Pickleball? Golf? Whatever it is, just get out there and have fun!

Time outdoors

Hiking, backpacking, and skiing are, of course, great sports that can really test the limits of your endurance. Most people that participate in those activities do so for a couple of reasons: (1) the great exercise benefits; and (2) the unbeatable exposure to the world's natural beauty. They're absolutely right on in their pursuit of those goals.

But what if you don't want to become an endurance athlete just to enjoy nature? You don't have to. The benefits of simply being outdoors in nature are unparalleled. Even if you live in the middle of the city, find time to sit on a park bench. Don't do anything but listen to the birds and watch the squirrels. Soak in a little sun. Let yourself get drenched by the rain. Make a snow angel. No matter the weather, a little time outdoors is undeniably good for you.

Indeed, there's a reason why even the most hardened prisoners still get an hour of outdoor time every day . . . our bodies and souls need that connection to nature. You may not think of yourself as a "nature girl" but I'm willing to bet that once you start spending time outdoors, you'll begin to crave it more and more. So, give it a try. What's the worst that can happen?

Coherence

I'm guessing that many of you haven't heard about "coherence." That's ok. I hadn't either before I started practicing it. Let's start by allowing the experts to define it for you:

"Coherence" is a term used by researchers to describe a highly efficient psycho-physiological state in which your nervous system, cardiovascular, hormonal and immune systems are working together efficiently and harmoniously.

Ultimately, it is a practice formed around the belief that your emotions have a big impact on the systems in your body. You know this to be true intuitively. Have you ever been so nervous or upset that you found your heart was racing? Have you ever caught a cold immediately after the stress of finals was over? Has your period ever come late when you were particularly nervous about something? All of this happens because your mind and your body were designed to work together.

You might have surmised, then, that coherence is the practice of focusing on different body systems—like your heartbeat or breathing— while simultaneously focusing on positivity in your life. In doing so, you can actually have a positive physical impact on those systems. I know, I know, it is a little complex to explain but the practice is actually quite simple. In fact, I suggest that you watch the video referenced in this footnote––– in order to get your bearings.

And, just in case you're tempted to blow this off as some hippie voodoo shit, you should know that even some of the world's hard-hitting scientists believe coherence is highly beneficial for your mind and body.

Last but definitely not least, masturbation

Yeah, okay. I said it. You have an amazing power that can bring you pleasure beyond comparison. Have you used it? I'm hoping, in today's day and age, that you all have. But I still know some women who haven't. And that's too bad.

Yes, I'm talking about masturbation. Self-love. Ménage à moi. DIY time. Jillin' off. You get the picture. A lot of women don't want to talk about it, but I'm not a lot of women. So let's take a look at some of the benefits of self-pleasure:

- Helps you relax
- Allows you to understand how you like to be pleasured
- Eases menstrual cramps
- Leads to better sex with a partner
- Helps you sleep better
- Relieves sexual tension
- Feels really good
- Feels super good . . . it was worth a second bullet point.

There are approximately 15,326 additional reasons why masturbation is good for you, but isn't this list enough? Look, I understand that some of you were raised to believe that it is wrong. Or dirty. Or against your religion. And I implore you in this moment to rethink where those confines came from. All you are doing is touching your own body. And creating pleasure. What could be more natural?

And . . . if you're really, really opposed to touching yourself, why not try something else that will touch you for pleasure? Maybe a vibrator (or a "back massager," if you're still fooling yourself) or (gasp!) a dildo? You can order these things online these days and no one will have to see your blushing (smiling) face while you order up your own well-being.

Look, this book is all about self responsibility and there is no better thing to hold yourself responsible for, than your own pleasure.

As I'm writing this, I believe 50% of you have already signed on to this plan and 50% of you are struggling with it. I've said all I can say on this topic. Go forth—enjoy, smile and glow.

Wrap up

So . . . what are you gonna do? I've now given you 12 different tools to enhance your mind, body, and soul. I wouldn't have presented you with any one of them if: (a) I hadn't personally tried it; and (b) benefitted from it. Now it's your turn.

To remind you of the challenge for this chapter, I want you to pick three of the above tools that you are going to practice regularly for 60 days. One should be for your mind. One should be for your soul. Once should be for your body. And remember, make those choices for yourself—not based on how I've characterized the tools above.

I'm not asking for a radical life change. I'm asking for 10 to 15 minutes per day. You can even alternate between your mind, body, and soul tools throughout the challenge period. (I suspect the time you spend doing this stuff will steadily sneak up).

At the end of each week that you commit to this practice, I want you to write down how each practice has changed your life. After the 60 days are up, go back and evaluate your whole journey. I promise you'll be enlightened. I'm betting one or more of these practices sticks with you for the rest of your days.

Good luck and have fun!

"What's the greatest lesson
a woman should learn?
That since day one, she's already had
everything she needs within herself. It's the
world that convinced her she did not."

—Rupi Kaur

Thirteen

You've ALWAYS Had Permission

Well, look at you! Wait! look at us! We both made it to the final chapter of the book. I don't know about you, but it has been a helluva journey for me. There have been tears, laughter, lessons, despair, joy, "ah-ha" moments, writer's block, frustration, anger, bliss, and everything in-between.

Indeed, even though I had a full outline for this book before I started writing it, I had no idea how much I would continue to learn as the words flowed from my head and heart onto the page. And now we're at that penultimate moment, the time when we're about to part ways and go on living our separate lives. At this moment, there's one question that I feel like I really need to ask you . . .

Do you feel like you need anyone's permission to go live your best life?

I sincerely hope and want to believe that your answer is a resounding "no." The purpose of this book was certainly not for me to give you permission to do anything. The purpose was for you to realize, as Rupi Kaur said, that you already had everything you needed within yourself.

The frustration comes with, "Yeah, that all sounds great but what the hell do I do with that?!?" It is my sincerest desire this book has given you the ways to explore how you have given up permission, and solid ways to grab it back again.

And, thus, what I hope I've ultimately given you is that knowledge—that confidence—to understand that everything you need really is within you. In fact, as I started to enter the state of grief that can sometimes come when you finish writing a book (just like the grief that comes when you finish reading a book that you love), I began to think, worry, ruminate:

Did I put everything I needed into this book? Did I give them everything they need to go out in the world and **not** ask for permission?

As I weighed these thoughts, the idea of "confidence" kept coming up. Because I realized that what I really wanted us all to walk away from this experience with was confidence to live your own lives.

So, guess what? The research nerd in me went and looked up the 10 greatest indicators of confidence. I found a great article from Forbes Magazine on that very topic.

Here are the things their writers tell us instill confidence:

- Getting things done.
- Monitoring your progress.
- Doing the right thing.
- Exercising.
- Being fearless.
- Standing up for yourself.
- Following through.
- Thinking long term.
- Not caring what others think.
- Doing more of what makes you happy.

Oh, girl! Don't you think you're going to check off all of those boxes if you just:

- Live with intention (Chapter 1).
- Be clear in your expectations from others and open to others' expectations from you (Chapter 2).
- Question and respectfully challenge the cultural confines that impact you (Chapters 3 and 4).
- Build strong relationships with yourself and others (Chapter 5).

- Temper your reliance on social media (Chapter 6).

- Carefully consider the professionals you hire to assist with your journey (Chapter 7).

- Recognize, embrace, and move past your victimhood (Chapter 8).

- Stand in your Mission Essential (ME) (Chapter 9).

- Be bold, always (Chapter 10).

- FailSpectacularly (Chapter 11).

- Tap into your innate supreme wisdom (Chapter 12).

My point is this: each of the chapters of this book is intended as a gift for you. Within each chapter lies the tools, exercises, and awareness you need to build your confidence, to rise from your lowest moment, and to move forward with grace and purpose. It is up to you to go forth and shine the light and love that is in you.

I have always thought of myself as being the youngest one in the room, not for the obvious ego reasons, but because I have always felt like I have so much to learn. Life is big and complicated and messy. Just when I thought I had it all figured out . . . queue the next lesson.

As I sit on the other side of this book, I feel like I have gained some hard-won wisdom. I knew I had ideas, insights, skills and experience that I wanted to share with you, but I had no idea that this book would so profoundly shift my perspective as well.

Of course, the act of writing the book held many lessons for me, but actually participating in and integrating the information had some surprising and wonderful benefits for my life and my outlook. As I breathe a sigh of relief, I am overtaken with emotion as our relationship comes to a natural end. But that really is the circle of life isn't it?

It's like the process I went through raising my girls. For 18 years I kept repeating myself (sometimes louder and louder), trying to give them everything I thought they would need in life. As they approached the time to leave the nest, I hoped I had given them the "right" tools but more importantly, I realized that these tools were going to change for them, in the way that they used them and applied them. They would have to figure out what worked best for them in the world to create their own best possible life—by their definition.

So, while I can pass on this knowledge, it is your responsibility to apply it in the way that makes the most sense for your life. Just as I came away a different person than I was when I started writing this book, it is my hope that you now have the tools to challenge yourself to be who you want to be. Every day we wake up and make a decision of how we want to show up in our own lives. You now have the tools to be intentional about your decisions.

I consider you all, in this bittersweet moment, my children. I don't care if you are 50 years younger than me or 50 years older. I have a deep sense of respect for you. You have stuck it out with me through this whole book, you have put up with my challenges and smart-ass comments and, hopefully, you came through the other side with a new profound sense of yourself.

That is really the point.

This is your life. Go live it and never, ever ask for permission.

Oh yeah . . . and call your mom once in a while!